Pearls
—that—
Shine
Poetry & Prose

Hank P. Luz

PARTRIDGE
A Penguin Random House Company

To order additional copies of this book, contact
Toll Free 800 101 2657 (Singapore)
Toll Free 1 800 81 7340 (Malaysia)
orders.singapore@partridgepublishing.com

www.partridgepublishing.com/singapore

This book *Pearls That Shine* is dedicated to my wonderful family, my loving wife, Shadah, my children Azlin, Hafidz, Azhar and their respective families, Norman, Kimie, Qaty, Nabil, Sara Ayesha and little Naqib. They are the inspiration and also the subject for many of the postings in my blog *Rainbow*

Acknowledgement

Pearls That Shine is a compilation of postings of poetry and prose from my blog *Rainbow* for the early months of 2013. I had earlier started blogging through *birdhouse* with writings in prose from June 2008

I wish to thank my family for their patience, tolerance and support in helping me to remember events and places in the course of my writings through the years. My thanks are also extended to my blogging friends who keep me company namely, eminent author and poet Ninotaziz and Akhi Norzah together with Pakcik Hassan, abdulhalimshah and Zam.

Last but not least to Jo and his team in Partridge for their untiring efforts in making *Pearls That Shine* a reality.

Contents

Introduction

My blogging days in *Rainbow* started with my responses to prompts from other poets who dedicated themselves to creating prompts on a regular basis. Invariably one can write a poem everyday as there are always prompts to goad us on.

Parts:

The writings in *Pearls That Shine* are organized into 5 parts according to their forms. A major portion is in the form of Free Verse and Haiku. Then Limericks, Micro Fiction but these are of a lesser number. The last part grouped under Forms for All are the rare ones of various forms but of a few postings.

Images:

Many of the poems have notations of images but there are no images accompanying them. The images are there in the blog postings in *Rainbow* but are deleted in the book for want of space. All pictures are either from Hank's collection or sourced from family members and friends. There are no images downloaded from the internet. All sketches and drawings are done by Hank himself or from Norman, Hank's talented grandson.

Prompts:

There is also a notation on prompts at the bottom of the page for some but none for others. In blogosphere one can google for background knowledge. But in *Pearls That Shine* this is not possible. The notations will therefore help to put some light into the background relevant in the poems. There are no notations if they are straight forward cases.

Part I

Free Verse

Free verse is close to normal speech. It is prose broken up with line breaks instead of punctuations and paragraphing. There is a tendency in contemporary poetry to use shorter lines

A Debutante

A debutante so alluring
Making an appearance
Susceptible to wild trivia
But unflinching by nature
Obliquely not connecting
Engaging rather shyly
Under extreme provocation

Where have the good guys gone?

Oblivious of hungry looks
Advancing cautiously
Amidst prying eyes
Stepping gingerly forward
With a come hither stance
Gliding with guarded precision
A lady for the offering
Sensuously intense

But where have all the good guys gone?

Patience

Attribution: Hank's Collections
Image: Hank with a whopper

It was late afternoon. The heat of
the day still beating down on us. The
sea was calm. The sky was clear in
bluish hues with white clouds drifting
leisurely by. It looked to be so inviting.
The beach was filled with the shrieks
and laughter of youngsters stragglers
from the crowd barely minutes ago
It would be quiet shortly with dusk
approaching.

We put out to sea in the middle of
the night. The heavens above was
full of twinkling stars. A slight sea
breeze playfully rocked the boat
a little.

We shone the torch-lights into the
crystal clear waters. That was one
way to attract the squids to the
surface which were scooped up
as bait

Light waves kept lapping the sides
of the boat to a regular rhythm.
It rocked us in time preventing
us from having a shut-eye.

The night was uneventful with
just small bites. The regular rocking
was a bother. It was frustrating
and the night was long

The break of dawn was the clincher.
Bites galore, what a whopper!

Night fishing was a test of patience
Saving the best for last!

Water Hyacinth

Attribution: Hank's collection
Image:1 The first bloom appeared on Jan 11, 2013

There were grass carp and cat-fish at different
times in the enclosure - a small pond-like thing
at the backyard. The heat was unforgiving and the
fish did not survive for long

A lean-to or a tiny top cover would be ideal
It needed shade. But the backyard was already
cramped. This option was not pursued. Something
to be done to the water surface was the alternative
This enclosure did not cover much space so it
should be easy

It all started with just two tiny stalks. These grew
very fast. They spread out with daughter-stalks
in all directions. I was the culprit who kept
throwing in of what were left of the old fish
feed in the initial stages. These acted as fertilizer
and spawned the growth faster.

On Jan 11, our 'little pond' sprung a surprise
A tiny flower stalk stole out the previous evening
I didn't think much of it. The next morning the
first ever blooms appeared - three little clumps.
The following day more appeared. It was exhilarating!

Water hyacinth is known to block waterways, clogging
the water surface. It prevents sunlight from reaching the
bottom that supports marine life. But for this
enclosure it is a controlled situation. It's all right!

I plan to stock the pond again with only the hardy
cat-fish to help ward off mosquitoes. The water is
cooler now with the surface cover. But I would have
to keep the growth and progress of the water hyacinth
in check.

Prompt:
The prompt calls for something on 'growing up'. It's
most opportune as it was a few months growing and
the first bloom appeared at the right time

Sunday, January 20, 2013

Retirement

One waits in anticipation for years
The day will dawn, have no fears

But in the meantime slog along
Do your own thing, and press on

Time and space hurtle past
Slowly in the beginning but then just

Amidst responsibilities are testing times
Governed by targets and deadlines

Time spent with co-workers and friends
Are often at the expense of quality time

Surviving and striving are part of the journey
To fend for themselves are woes of the family

Cruel but a necessary element of change
Open to failings on occasions of pain

Mistakes and blurred decision-making
Are rampant in an environment of working

Of mistakes not material, a consolation
But rectification can restrain advancement

All in chasing and overcoming odds
The rat race is often an unforgiving lot

Looking forward to days of retirement
To be rid of all the pressures and deadlines

Ironically though, retirement can be boring
The experience of those before us is telling

Unfortunately wisdom comes a tad too late
Nonetheless one ought to be more prepared

Some very clever ones were to the fore
Prepared for retirement but busier than before

Bliss

The world whirled slowly by
Medley of forms and activities
Some accepted some on the sly
And many others of mediocrity

Many who planned to procure
Executed them with perfection
But some just failed to endure
Unashamedly await for salvation

Oblivious to what transpired
The outside world was no bother
Adhering to whims and desires
Young couples aligned their rudder

In a world of their own venture
Holding hands, pitching a wish
Time stood still pristine in nature
Have we elders not savored such bliss?

Prompt:
A picture prompt of a
couple holding hands

Why?

Elusive and mysterious
Lurking in the shadows
Where Art Thou, Creativity?
Show yourself, let me see

Unflagging faith in your presence
Loyalty unquestioned
We've been through together
Why aren't you here?

Where are you
This won't do
Hear my plea
It's plain to see

It used to come easy
Just you and me
Whether in writings
or in sketchings

Now it's kind of slow
And I'm on a low
It's a shock
Yet again the old Writer's Block!

The News

It's a slow death
As of many others
It has always been there
Keeping one company
An early morning ritual
But its days are numbered

Just as a portly gentleman
Anorexia nervosa afflicted
Thinning and wasting away
A predicament no less

No more throws-in over
the gates nor news-vendors
Nor news vending machines
A paper-less society making
an invisible presence

A pity for the 'papers magnate
That controlled the print media
Their empire crumbled
Whittled down drastically
They lost their influence

Or is it? No it is not!
A resilient lot with the old adage
'You can't fight them you join them'
So they too are in cyberspace

Currently extending free offerings
Perhaps devising a foolproof system
To get at that odd few cents

31

of our newspaper money
They used to get before

In time we'll be made to pay
For the news we crave everyday!

Pop Music

The 50's and 60's were hailed as the greatest era
of pop music. The baby boomers came of age.
A whole generation of young people appeared
on the music scene. Support of this generation
and youngsters following them spawned myriads
of musical forms and famous pop stars

There were rock n roll greats in Chuck Berry and
Bill Hayley. Followed by Elvis, Cliff Richard, Ricky
Nelson, Paul Anka and Connie Francis. Groups
likewise began to make an appearance with The
Beatles, Rolling Stones, Beach Boys, Temptations
and the Supremes

The Beatles created a sensation with their
particular brand of music. Their presentation
of dressing, peculiar form and sound shocked
rock n roll into submission

Nothing prepared the music scene though when a
whole generation found themselves gyrating to
Chubby Checker's, the Twist. Some minor ones like
limbo rock tried to cash in on the madness but it
did not make an impact. Despite all these, individual
stars of evergreens with the likes of Frank Sinatra

Tom Jones, Andy Williams, Johnny Mathis and a host
of other notable ones kept those who thrived in the
sentimental offerings going.

But nothing shocked the world when Michael Jackson
went solo from the Jackson Five and held sway
transcending the generation gap. He mesmerized
everyone with his new form (characterized by the
moonwalk and others that typically were identified
with him)

With his passing, the music world was lost in its
bidding and hungry for someone to fill the gap. It
grabbed at Psy's Gangnam Style recently but just
how long will that last!

Wednesday, January 30, 2013

Questions, questions!

Of a *drab* rainy night
A weather unkind for wants
Lashed against all its might
Could it force itself out front?

One's head dashed reeling
Pulsating of spiral dreams
Compounded of acts troubling
Must it occur to extremes?

Frustrations turned for the worst
Tendrils entwined the mind's undone
Save the cause of strength first
Would they fall in place for once?

33

Prompt
To include the words:
drab pulsate tendrils

A Raintree

Note: There was a row of tall raintrees in my old
neighborhood which must have been about 80 years
by now. They were already there for as long as I
could remember. They were still standing though
some made way for development.

Casting a net on the outset
Barely on the outskirts of imagination
Amidst a pall of outward intrusion
A smokescreen of shadowy apparition

Pungent in a quaint whiff of cool breeze
Purporting of quiet movements
In intermittent bright and dark shadows
The swarthy old raintree extending
a canopy over the neighborhood

Unabated it stood tall and menacing
In sudden bright sunshine or drab stupor
Smirking in light smog and drowsiness
A shrewd measure of strength

A Library

You look spiky for the whole world to see
Mayhem of construction works manifold
Mandated from 2010 till two-zero-one-three
Man had decided that you remained closed

Considering you had been around since 1934
Old age demands to restore moments of splendor
There are enough reasons to thwart the specter
The indignity of refurbishment you are to undergo

Thus once again to the masses of Manchester
To emerge vibrant and to rally unflinching enthusiasm
Of a service and facility sturdy without stutter
The City Fathers had taken the momentous decision

Fervent in educating the enthusiastic youngsters
Sober adults, golden oldies, with hopes of sincerity
In all those good old fashioned reading ventures
Modernized facilities to maintain its 'structural integrity'

Prompt:
A picture prompt of Manchester Library
which was being renovated

That's Greed

It's embarrassing to say the least
When caught with their pants down

With connivance they expect a feast
Determined to scrounge so profound

No qualms about making an assertion
Such poor taste one cannot readily fathom
When without batting an eyelid they fashioned
Ways and means to get even

Ways of the world are plain indeed
Outwitting the unsuspecting and uninformed
Easy way out and fostered by greed
But it'll catch up and backfire that's the norm

Prompt:
To include the words *embarrass taste backfire*

Loving You!

You had sounded so tense and desperate
I rushed over here when I got your tweet
What's up? I told myself not to be late
Nothing pressing I thought we should meet

I'm really so glad nothing's the matter
You had me worried for one brief moment
Been meaning to call but something or other
Got in the way that got me off tangent

I thought we agreed to meet in a few days
That was the reason why I was so afraid
I'm sorry Honey, I was aware but as I laze
thoughts of you swirled wildly in my head

Best we meet I decided to call you anyway
I just can't wait to call you this time
I know it may just be another few more days
But I'll kiss anyway for Happy Valentine!

Prompt:
Happy Valentine

Sacrifices

Decisions defying reasoning
Often circumstances demand
Done with precision fulfilling
Spontaneous but irrational

How to explain sexual cannibalism
of the Black Widow eating its mate
after mating. The reverse is true
in suttee. Self immolation of a widow
at her husband's funeral pyre

The ultimate sacrifice!

Diving kamikaze pilots and harakiri
disembowelment performed by the
samurai. Heroic acts accepted and
revered by their society. If only
good sense prevailed in place
of dogged patriotism

Some things were best left
unsaid for their reasons were
beyond reasoning!

Prompt - *sacrifice*

Curiosity

A house far out the country-side
Ignited a curiosity in one's mind
Abandoned but mysteriously prone
to frequent probes of unseen visitors
Tyre marks visibly awkward but in abundance
From the gates to the house and back
But oddly enough avoiding a drive through
where an open gate offered least resistance
But strangely no one took the route

A white car stuck in the mud for
as long as one could remember
None so brave as to venture out to see
Heard say there were four occupants
who refused to exit and were now skeletons

Basking in the heat of summer
Shriveled in the cold of winter
as if huddling close together for warmth
Eerie and frightening, no one dared
to take a peek but rather letting
the many mysterious visitors to keep
their secret with a discovery morbid
or otherwise, no one cared to question!

38

Prompt
Picture prompt of of a lone house
on a hill. The gates were wide open
but there were no tyre marks. Indication
that no one had passed through them.
There was a white car stuck in the
mud in the compound

A Destroyer

The fabric of life's macabre vision
Expounding its will on the morrow
Threatened they scrambled for positions
Not to pulsate in throes of sorrow

Embroidery set in sophisticated patterns
Salient in rough skins of colors so loud
Seldom to malign strong lyrics in rhythm
Character prim with extraordinary clout

Can life so planned to wield such power
A creature with sentiments all set to sire
Satiated with elements regal in nature
Pandemonium unleashed to emerge destroyer

Prompt
embroidery-

Graffiti

Seen at strategic locations
No more just at the outskirts
Right in mid-town spots
Opening up to the freedom of expression
Which may appear strange at the outset

It's outrageous!
It's not palatable!
It's humorous!
It's bawdy!
Outright obscenity!

Blatant disregard of accepted norms
The palette in hand running wild

Do they serve a purpose?
Yes!

City fathers accompanied by local authorities
Can take a look-see
Even a cursory glance sufficed
of graffiti all over the city
of what's ailing in the locality

Lack of facilities
Level of poverty low
Employment setbacks
Profusion of delinquency
Illegal immigrants wanting to be heard

Supplementing graphs, figures or write-ups
solutions may not be to the dot

Accuracy is not the objective
But the big picture can tell a thousand words

Apparently the preponderance of graffiti
on bathroom walls is indication of frustrations
outside the walls!

Is this true!

Hustled

To the kitchen he headed
But it broke his little heart
He spied a visual he dreaded
He reacted with starts

How could he disclose
what he had found
Sure for now it was not his boast
His room-mate had gone

Juxtaposed on the table
Plates on the ready he assumed
But alas, none of the edibles
He had brought home to consume

He lost, it was one down
A fatal mistake he quipped
Should have tucked in
earlier he frowned
His buddy rifled the grub
when he fell asleep

He was left with no food
Not a fair bid

Prompt:
Picture of an empty plate

A Lady's Plea!

Ganging up on the lady
Is it that easy!
Whose idea is that!
Covered with drawers!!

Conveniently
attached at my strategic knocks
and right places
Sacrilege!
I'm better off without
just my arms
That's all!
That's how I'm always seen
It cannot be any better
That's how I've always been

Shatter-proof glass luxury
Mona Lisa had it easy
But short end of the stick for me
Glaringly
homesickness gnawing
on my raw nerves
Begging you!
Please take me back
Take me back to the Louvre

Venus belongs there too
Not just Mona!
Do you hear!
Do you dare!
You gentlemen care?

Prompt:
Statue of Venus de Milo
Covered with drawers

Dry Humor

A fabric of like feelings
Feigning a laughter of sorts
Illicit in its nature
Patterned by a show of pranks
Precursor of base humor
Ravenous in its desire
to cause glee but lacking witticism
Reckless stimulant to stricken pride
Exhausted in its bid
to stoop so low
to torment
those not led to
enjoy some chuckles
the straight faced
the serious
those unworthy
of vibrant nature
to just trudge along
with no sparkle in life

Innocence

Young hearts of innocence
Little things mean a lot
Taking them all at face value
That words sweetly uttered
Bound feelings of love

But he left…
Not without reasons
But just
But why?

Tolerance spread thin
It's a disappointment!
Left in the lurch
Strings unattached
All alone in this cruel world
Cared less and abandoned
Why must she be made to suffer
Her heart shattered into a million pieces
Left in the cold
Drenched to the skin

No, mankind hadn't been hurting
Humankind wasn't at fault
It's all about him and him alone

I'm young
I'm pretty
I'm strong!

Faith in a good man
Hadn't waned

It's a blessing
I'm now better prepared
My tears shed but I've learnt

I'll overcome!
A good man is waiting
Somewhere.

Unlimited Wants

By way of wants
The yearnings of yonder
That's not how it had all begun
The wonder of wonders

Unlimited wants
Unlimited yearnings
Care for a show?

Scarcity all whims
Creating demands unsurpassed
Grinds the wheel moving
Feed them in the past

Adam Smith leads the way
Born of the Wealth of Nations
Held spell-bound, held sway
Right on with the actions

Principles and theories
Come into play in absolute terms

45

Not creating worries
But providing answers and solutions

Economics had been fun
Satisfying unlimited wants!

Moths

A species nocturnal in nature
Fluttering in the cool breeze
Of a right feel delicate in stature
Not groping in the very least

Conversant of life in the dark
Not active but graceful in movements
Skirting tree to tree bark to bark
Sedentary a while at some moments

Idyllic setting none so right
But for predators lurking in wait
May upset the quiet of the night
Caught in a skirmish and left for dead

Slow moving life forms bear the danger
Elements of the animal world's way of attrition
Risks of transfer from one perch to the other
Brutal but bears witness of natural occurrence

Prompt:
To include the following words in a verse:
grope transfer brutal

At a Loss!

He is still at a loss
He thought he had it made
It all seemed too easy
None as to be that complicated
She had said 'yes'
He had known her that long

Now this!
Why?
Why did she change her mind?

Standing at the crossroads
This is a challenge
He has learnt that much
about her to know her
He has to bid his time
He has to give her time
It is only fair
She had gone through so much herself
He had not been that
easy a guy to be with
It was easy before
But not now

He'll be fair
He'll give in this time
Afterall Mom knows best
And she is the best Mom!

Peace so elusive!

A very quiet beach
Devoid of human forms
Early morning mist
Nor other animal movements

Except for the slow lashing
of the lazy waves on the shore
In the distance glistening
As a glass sheet crystal clear

Peaceful as it is!

The same cannot be said
Of what's around the local scene
The crime wave driving us mad
Of profiteers ever so mean

It's no better globally
Power play against the weak
Those not affected take it lightly
'Not in my backyard' we play it meek

Peace clamored for!

The beach is ever so peaceful
Semblance of regulated nature's ways
Not readily offered in a world of plentiful
Where greed and high handedness held sway

Peace so elusive!

Nature's Wrath

Provocatively dark
Swirling in motions not likely
to find a solution
Turbulent skies
Pugilistic

Uncharitable, undeterred
Volatile in its make up
Ready to unleash
the power within

Underlings on earth
Preparing a defense
Against an expected
stormy encounter

The Heavens falling!
Be it snow, rain, hailstones
Blizzards and sandstorms
The Heaven's warning!
Volcanic eruptions, earthquakes
and tsunami

Global warming!
Retribution demands
a correction to ills of human folly

Repent!

Flowers

Flowers that will not wait
for the snow to steal away
its strength, its fate
sealed when led astray

Likeness of *adaptations*
Clusters of low brush
Twisted in its elation
Taking the *silent roar of the vast*
wooded jungle of *thorn saplings*
Stout-stemmed twisted but strong
slowly, *zigzagging*

A picture of sensibility
To survive, *stealing the sun*
to glow in a phony
protocol of the wayward son

Flowers that *employ the wind*
To garner support to retain
its beauty, an outright sin
but for a good cause without restrain

A thing of beauty
In all its tenacity!

Prompt:
To use a given Botanical wordlist
and phrases (in italics)to use in a poem

Who am I?

Looks can be deceiving
You may not have seen me
But my reputation precedes me
You would have heard of me
It's all attributed to my looks

You probably would have conjured
something different. I've been thought
to be very beautiful not that I'm not. But
I've been known to be brightly and
loudly colored. Splashes of green, red
and blue are generously part and
parcel of my kind. I'm known to hunt
for my keeps in that unusual way
I hunt not on land nor do I consume
little insects or berries. I go for the
big kill, sometimes bigger than me.
And another thing! I'm not a swimmer
but I can zero in and dive into murky
waters to get what I want

Look at me!
You think
what am I?

Yes, I'm a kingfisher from the Amazons and this
is how I look. Not that colorful but a
kingfisher no less.

Prompt:
A picture prompt of a kingfisher but
not so colorful

Cracks

Get cracking, go for it!
Get moving crack the whip

But crackpots crave for some fun
Smoking crack a tragedy in the sun
Cracking software a test of wills
Cracked copies risking the bill
Crack a code
That's a big load
Crack at the job
Shows a big flop
Crack a safe
Not nicely made
A crack shot
Is all that's required

Not cracking under pressure
Lawyers knocking at the defendant's composure

Driving's a real pleasure
If not cracking 70 miles per hour
Crackdown on speeding
To rope them in

At the crack of dawn
Lots of movements
Cracking the time
To earn a living
A crack shot with lots of potential
Crack at the job is very essential

Crack in the head working like a dog
And cracking up from overwork

Prompt:
Write anything on 'cracks'

A Kamishibai

Image Deleted
A Catamaran

Note: A Kamishibai was a traveling story-teller of old Japan who made his rounds going from village to village with stories many in the form of a haibun. A haibun is a prose together with a set of haiku.

Note: 2 The catamaran we were on was similar complete with sails. We were given a 20 mins instruction on safety before putting out to sea. It was very necessary as it was fast and it was open. I had then just been awarded a Bronze Medallion a life savings medal which made me a qualified life-saver. So it was ok for me.

I now wish to recount what a thrilling experience I had through a haibun.

The Prose
This happened many years ago when I was
just a 16 year old school boy. Our school was
by the sea. Capt Preedy who was on the faculty
was a sea-faring naval officer who owned a
catamaran. It was stored in a shed by the sea-side

One Sunday, I was fortunate enough to have
volunteered together with one other to help
out at the shed. After some cleaning and
clearing chores, Capt Preedy decided to
take the catamaran out to sea. Surprises
of surprises, the 2 of us were invited on
board. It was such a thrill!

It was as fast as a speed boat depending on
the wind then. It was more risky as it was
open. We could be thrown into the water so
a life jacket was mandatory

We were taken for a spin not far from shore for
quite some time (I don't quite remember
how long now) I had been on a boat, sampan,
and raft, (later a kayak at the Outward Bound
School)

But nothing beats a catamaran!

The Haiku
Such excitement! A
catamaran ride never
forgotten. Such bliss!

The wind brushing the
cheeks. Wisps of hair in
the face and the eyes

Salt water splashing
everytime it hits the waves
It was so thrilling!

Future Twin Godfathers

Moments in time of varied capture
Fleeting through in a blinding flash
Or tip-toeing slowly for all at leisure
In between a quick and random dash

Moments in time of aggressive runs
Surreptitiously vying for some privacy
Crude may it seem but two young guns
Creating a power base in all simplicity

Moments in time of a street fighter
Who had to survive with his wits intact
Scrimping and looking for the better
Instinct his weapon strong as yet

Seeing double is a worked out decoy
Reflection here is a planned deception
Terrible twins are known to destroy
To achieve the duo's wicked ambitions

Prompt:
Picture prompt of two young
men dressed as hoodlums

No. #1

No. #1!
Everybody take notice

Been lots of fun!
A slight hiccup but nothing's amiss
I'm staking my claim
for my numero uno
I've been away lately
but not any more

Now I've got it back!
It's sweet seeing all others
Vying for the same
It's all in the game
One has to go for it
Fun of winning
Is not an easy thing
It may be a little pain
But there are lots of gain
One must have the *passion*
With all the gumption
Of a champion

No. #1! No.# 1!
It sure is fun!
I'm back!
Don't forget that!

Gleefully these are perhaps
what ran through his mind
Words befitting of a sports icon
Tiger Woods has returned
to the top of world ranking
Tiger replaces Rory Mc Illroy
As World No.1 when he won
The Arnold Palmer Invitational
Over the week-end!

Elvis the King

Twins Jesse Garon Presley and Elvis Aaron Presley
were born on Jan 08 1935 but the elder Jesse
was still-born. Elvis went on to be 'The King'
and dominated the world music scene

He had wanted a bicycle or a gun for his birthday
But he got a guitar, a less costly alternative

But what a blessing it was and music was not
the same since

'That's All Right' reportedly meant for his mother's
birthday topped the charts and opened the way
for others beginning 1953. Inspired by Bill Hayley's
Rock Around the Clock which was No.1 on the Charts
in 1954 he never looked back. What masterly
good fortune that he found 'rock and roll' bursting
onto the scene at the same time as that of his singing.

Blessed with good looks and the African-American
voice of Rhythm and Blues, the music world was at
his bidding. By 1956 he had 8 singles as No.1 on the US
Charts. Among the notable ones were Heartbreak Hotel, Don't
Be Cruel, Hound Dog, Love Me Tender and All Shook Up

Riding on his popularity, he got onto the silver screen
with Love Me Tender (1956) Jailhouse Rock (1957) and
Blue Hawaii (1961) More hits on the Charts and more films
followed. His gyrations on stage and young girls swooning
at Elvis the Pelvis (a handle he abhorred) kept the 60's and
70's on high. But 'on high' at this time was not just a buzz word
but also a bad word in the entertainment world. The drug scene

initially seen as an exclusive and accepted phenomena later
was viewed with disdain and condemned many talented
artists into oblivion and early death.

Most unfortunately The King was no exception. Prescribed by his
physician it meant it was ok to Elvis. It was thought to be so! But
not so.

He was more depressed when his former bodyguards who
had close access to him wrote a tell-all book on his drug habit

Elvis was found comatose on his bed on Aug 16 1977 apparently
following a heart attack brought on by drug abuse for a long period
of time. It was most unfortunate that it happened at a young age of 42

Despite that he could still top the charts posthumously with
singles JailhouseRock (2002) One Night (2005) and
It's Now or Never (2005) among others!

Hail the King!

The reason why mothers are invented

Nature's way of ensuring life's being
Baby's wailings are sure signs of
either the diapers need changing
or hunger is forcing an issue

Moms, the mobile kitchen are always
at hand. Mom comes running to appease anger
Infants are spared of pangs of hunger
But not for long as change of diet
requires a proper kitchen besides

breast-feeding, warmth and loving care
Early in life the kitchen is seen as an
unequalled savior in the household,
a sanctuary for mothers to hone her culinary
skills, useful in the long run to ease off from
breast-feeding, or to whip up a quickie snack
for the growing-up years and to stack up the
'fridge and warmers ready for the fast moving
teenagers. All the while in the background
though, expectation is high from the head of the
household who may sometimes be more
demanding. An intelligent lady ought to
make adjustments to keep the cries of
empty stomachs addressed and within wraps

That's the reason why mothers are invented
and kept busy!

Note:
Apologies. Can't thank mothers enough
for being there when we need them!

Wednesday, April 3, 2013

A Speed Fiend

Half *squinting* blinded by the lights
and not really aware of a near miss

It could have been a disaster if not for
his quick reflects. It's hazardous and
risky for one to be on the road alone
these days. It wears one off! If there is no
valid reason to move around in the night
arguably it's a better option to just stay

home where one is king

Practically everyone else on the road
is in a hurry, day or night. A dangerous
overtaking just barely a few minutes ago
and one meets him at the next stop
sitting pretty enjoying a cool drink
Worst it may be a mangled wreck
that one meets if they have not
been careful.

No reason why they need to risk their
necks and throw caution to the winds
If they need to show they can *lick* everyone
else with their prowess behind the wheel
do so without endangering others. Joining a
club of like interest with others can be
an outlet to let off steam

Otherwise it's a mockery of the saying
'the good die young'

Prompt:
To include the words *squint argue lick*
in a verse

An Irony of Life

It is going to fun, I know it will

A contributor to the organization
For umpteen years, rose up the ladder
Knowledge abound and knowledge extended

Rewarded for the faith in serving
an employer of a gem

Given to appreciating good attitudes
and in return were facing challenges
together as a team

He had given his all as a model employee
He would be retiring and no more tensions
No more deadlines, no more office politics
No more bother and he was going to be free!

Hooray! Lots of freedom
My time is all for myself
Hooray! I'm far from all the drudgery

So he thought!

He had retired now for 3 months
It was heavenly, no worry
He had built up a modest nest egg
He would go for a pleasure cruise
Travels, see the world
Do his own thing!

He remembered it very well
It was fun when it lasted
But only for a month after retirement

He suddenly felt bored
The challenges he had before
were no more. He felt restless
Got in the way of others
much to the point of a nuisance
He almost gave up on life
until one day, his loving spouse

who saw the predicament
came by to him and said

'You have lots of time on your hand
You thought retirement can take it all
Retirement can, but only to a point'

What an irony! Being free but being bored

His loving spouse then came up with a brilliant suggestion
'Why not start blogging?'

Yes, so it is!

The Bard

Note: With sincere apologies to the Bard

All the world's a stage-coach, let's rob it!
Try to become a modern day Robin the Hood
Take some but share out the rest of the loot
All will be happy all parties benefiting
Isn't it the crass and nature of sharing?

To be, or not to be, that is not ***the question***
The question is to decide outright and act
The strength of purpose and will to crack
Will goad others to muster their courage
And move the world on a faster pace

But, for my own part, it is Greek to me
Flair for language brings it to a higher level
Prompting others to try and dabble

Swahili or Urdu are just as beautiful
As English or American are just as useful

The course of true love never did run smooth
Hustlers abound at every corner is a concern
Preying on the gullible and the innocents
Hard-hearted and mean the order of the day
Young or old, hustlers do not choose their prey

O Romeo, Romeo! wherefore art thou
Forever the bayings of a love-sick cow
Never seem to learn but betrayed by all
Frustrated and angry having missed the buck
But still insisting on pushing their luck

Prompt:
To write something Shakespearean

'to carry on'

To carry on right through
Doing things they normally do
Not to be outdone by distractions
Affecting one's traction
beyond!

Say, like walking early morning
Savoring the cool of the surrounding
Extending the feel of freedom
Pushing the mind
beyond!

The chirping of birdsongs
Rekindling, righting the wrongs
A melody in the brush
Not asking so much
Are we not able
Not to be saddled
With irritants
Bugging our minds
beyond?

Man with his idiosyncrasies
Forever in a crisis
Amid questions and confusion
Clawing for solutions
Life with all its permutations
Leading on and to carry on
beyond!

Prompt:
'to carry on..'

Honey

Honey, ever so sweet
Never missing breakfast
together just two of us
It's heavenly, it's blissful

Ever like two young lovers
rekindling back the old flames
of love nurtured through the years
Never another moment to match

What do we have here?
Honey and toast the most
healthy of foods don't you think!
Yes, nectar of sorts of varied flowers

Regurgitation and evaporation
A process acted through the ages
The hard working honey bees
In honeycombs storing them as honey

Human kind with all good intentions
Rob them of their nature's best
But they slave and slog still on
Injustice not a restriction

Visual Satisfaction

Image: Hank's sketch of a bamboo
cut done a few minutes ago

Note: Chinese painting or Japanese ink painting always fascinate me but apparently they're that technical. Special paper and brushes are very necessary to start with.
Ordinary drawing paper and the normal brushes as done above lacks the desired effects.

Is it a myth not to be aware of one's desires
Is it not reality to take control of one's yearnings
Strength that is ingrained within
Needs a twitch and a tickle to notice
Often without realizing and often at odd times
Comes a time in one's life
At that moment of peace and quiet
Of savoring tranquility and moments
Where one desires to be left alone
To find an idyllic setting

A profound realization of suddenness
On whatever pretext to fulfill an urge
To do one better and find solace

A whiff of inspiration engulfs
It creates an onslaught
That overwhelms

Time constraints present less restrictions
The wee of the morning or the heat of afternoon
It tugs at the conscience to take to paper and pencil
For an immediate reaction is vitally necessary
Lest it just disappears into thin air

Note it down in that little note-book
Sketch it on something tangible not in one's mind
For there's a treasure trove waiting to be tickled
From the abyss in the subconscious to reality
Poets, artists or any creative mind

Will need to succumb to the call
Or it'll be lost forever

Come With Me!

Come with me, I said
We've had it all made
Just you and me
Venture across the country
Foster feelings of fraternal ties
With kins we bade good-bye
Long ago when we sought
To venture forth abroad
To seek our fortune
Which was then the norm

Come with me, I said
You remember the fate
Of those who had cold feet
Not wanting to make a bid
To change their life-style
But to stay on awhile
Which later turned to years
After which they discard the urge
To ever venture out again
Not wanting to try and gain

Come with me, I said
The plans had been laid
Visions of wealth bountiful
Picked at ease plentiful
Stand up and be counted
Garner all the efforts

The strength of purpose
Made up without rehearse
To make a bold stand
All set to implement

Come with me, I said
It just couldn't wait!
Let's pay them a visit!

Prompt
To use the phrase *'Come with me, I said'*

The Fruit Gatherer

The fruit of knowledge is stuck all over
The fruit gatherer is the one who is observant
In picking out what she sees are better
Though sometimes may not be that relevant

But just the same she picks them up anyway
The kind of knowledge may not be needed then
It does not really matter, just pick them up everyday
To store away for use for later events

The danger is when she moves around with eyes shut
Not knowing or bothering either way of things around
It's regressive for to progress on is not to end up a dud
Losing out on knowledge that are likely to be found

Not unlike a zombie or an uncaring robot
For she is a thinking and functioning being

If only she makes it a point to walk about
With eyes open, sensitive to what she's seeing?

Prompt:
Picture prompt of a fruit gatherer

Come what may!

The dreamy faraway look
attesting to something that
is on his mind

What can be so damning,
so worrying, so as to put brakes
on his attention span

He is determined to let bygones be bygones
It is not to cause him to
lose sleep. It wore him off before
but not this time

By now he can already anticipate
Come what may!

But what is eating her
There are times he asked himself
Can he go on like this?

He is short of revealing the episode
But it is not him to *rekindle* the old hurts
The old wound might just fester
and get out of sync without a switch

It had involved third parties before
Those dear to his heart
He can't afford to extend the reach
There cannot be a miss!

There must be a finality
Come what may!

Prompt:
To use the phrase - *come what may*

Hurt

It hurt him bad
She felt it too
Not a big spat
But what could she do

Her mother was too harsh
She felt it also
Was mean for her to ask
Her hubby to just 'go'

What was it with her mom
Against him she couldn't fathom
He thought she should not be alone
So she visited her mother's home

But her mom had the heart to decide
To ask them to smoke outside!
She had just been a week as his bride
She too sacrificed to be by his side

70

What Choice?

Image (deleted)
Demonstration and a protest

On his own volition he left them
He had debated the various issues
He just could not reconcile his conscience
Tried as he did he questioned his dues

In the face of and against all norms
With a heavy heart he walked on

It was already a week into submission
It tugged at his person, was it fair?
What about the others in the coalition
He did not keep track he was not aware

He did not care as it wore off his energy
He gave his all why must they be so edgy?

It was a long while that he wracked his brain
On reflection, in all velleity he softened his hard-line
He thought of giving in to knock at his stance
He might when he could counter his firm stand!

It was a long haul but let it be he eventually decided
In the first place they should not have been one-sided!

Prompt:
To use the words - *volition and velleity*

A Crushing Blow

The given words:
cut opaque nebulous breathe timings
notched crushing blazing untouched
hovering bleak torch slab

He was a *cut* above the rest
so he believed. But an *opaque* squint
on his *nebulous* past kept haunting
him. He did not dare *breathe* a word
on his otherwise unblemished record

His reflects were perfect, his *timings*
were good. He *notched* winnings
with *crush*ing blows to his opponents.
He came with fists *blazing*. He had *visions* of
a great champion. He was un*touch*ed

But the stigma kept *hovering* over his head
It cast a *bleak* future over designs of
him as a *torch* bearer of his generation
It was a mistake of the past that kept
tripping him. After all it was just a *slab*
of fix a small portion that would not cause
real harm, not much anyway

Sadly, a sordid episode was not easily forgotten
by the fraternity. An icon with no tainted past
was expected no less which he could not fulfill
A slight baggage on his young shoulders kept
gnawing on his ambitions.
It broke his little heart

The Keeper

Happy as a lark swooping and gliding
The morning sun a partner all day in play
Of all kinds and sizes enjoying the morning
All day all night shrieking without a care

Such is life outside so free without restrictions
The eagles and hawks surveying the horizon
The migratory birds and sea-gulls in abundance
But not of the light-house keeper a lone occupant

The beginning of today is akin to yesterday's dawn
So it'll be for the rest of the day morning till dusk
By extension it is no different the whole of the month
The uneventful life of a lonely soul then and in the past

No ordinary folk can match the dedication
A responsibility of a true mariner's portfolio
A lonely life all alone and one of deprivation
Taken for granted for which not many may know

The swaying of the dandelion in the light breeze
Is the only living thing within the keeper's reach

Prompt:
A picture prompt of a light-house
with dandelions in the foreground

Layers of Flow

The layers of wellness rightly transformed
Pandering to the whims of a kind soul
Paving a flow of goodness with a penchant
For the well-being of a loving couple
A flow that fulfills the yearnings of a heart

A paragon of honor extending an olive branch
Hunger of a kind slaving for a morsel of truth
What can the response be if not one so blunt
Of a somber disregard yet one ever so smooth
A flow that yields a rhapsody of brilliance

Can one be expected to solicit for sympathy
Lest one is snubbed for being overly lavish
Let the truth be stamped with words of solidarity
Soothing the wild feelings contrary to one's wish
A flow that tugs at the turbulence of tyranny

Prompt:
The word - flow

Flowers

Note: Tulips apparently are edible

Does one ever realize it
The wonder of flowers
The appeal is explicit

To many of our senses

It's sweet and aromatic
A base for perfumery
Aroma by name specific
Supporting an industry

Its appeal to sight
Of brilliant colors
A darling of right
For palettes and cameras

Taste is another factor
Busy bees able to confirm
In their quest for nectar
A life giving form

Taste is not confined to bees
Humans take to consume
Tulips among others is believed
As edible and can be taken

Not forgetting the feel
To touch and savor its body
Delicate but a kiss can seal
Any mishandling impropriety

What if the world is devoid of flowers
It would be just greenery without colors

The wild truth

Gnawing at one's conscience
Not wanting to forget
Not just yet
But it's been building up slowly
Strongly by the day
Every which way

Time to make amends hold it by the horns
Ask for the reason why
Look it in the eye

Answers aren't forthcoming, why this is so
Was it too entrenched?
Let's take aim

Never to provoke a bear in hibernation
Not to poke a bee hive
So learn to survive

A strong boost
It's not a ruse
Make the most
Nothing to lose!
The wild truth!

Prompt:
Use the phrase - *the wild truth*

Lure of Wealth

Truckloads of sand transported
A determination well exhorted
Across the beaten tracks destined
For one man to stamp his dreams

A plot of land in the city limits
Of boisterous youngsters who forfeit
their time to share with friends
Now faced with land laid barren

First phase of plans now seeing reality
Pushing his luck in keeping with a fraternity
A developer bent on meeting a quirk of a decision
Of a partner in trade, the greedy politicians

For all to view to a build up of infamy
Of unscrupulous elements bent on money
At the feelings of loss of the community
Of a park deprived, loss of greenery

A Calling

The given words:
close connect anchored fertile range current
yield heart phrase shift beam hazy

An activist ever since the day
A close friend let him down at his

Most vulnerable moment

He was trying to connect through
Layers of relationships with those
Sharing like aspirations with him

He anchored his being and his cause
To a fertile range of current bidders
Intending to yield nothing

The phrase, heart of gold raised the
Possibility of achieving a shift and
A beam of hope to the poor

He was forever grateful to the friend
Who had unwittingly opened a door
For him to pursue his calling

He could see what was coming through
A smoke screen in the like of a hazy
Ponytail floating leisurely in the air

Sunday, May 26, 2013

A Couple

Oil and water
Enjoined together
Pushed to encircle
Together to grapple
With hues of colors
Waiting for an upsurge

Uphill leisurely moving
Slow uptake as most teams

Unsung but revealing
Unrepentant but slyly testing
Uncharted waters
Tainted by others
Tarnished and in tatters

A partnership is sacred
Make amends salvage an honor
Courage in valor
A loving couple all sensible
Not to expect a miracle
But just be exceedingly pliable

Good-bye

Good-bye, sayonara, au revoir
Say it whatever
which way whichever
It means tears not laughter

Can one be faulted
Emotions goaded
not evolved but immediate

Why just saying it invokes sadness
Why is separation so revealing
That tears go streaming
Is there no drama in between?

Till we meet again!
We may or may not meet
That is why

79

In the meanwhile
tears run dry
The feelings are sustained
It is difficult to explain
Tears of joy may just drop
Or of sadness unprompted
It is that difficult to say goodbye?

Authority Stifled

Wearing a badge of authority
Not wanting to appear inhibited
He weaved his way in the cool of the night
Seemingly doing the job of an enforcer
He tried his best to forget his inability
To haggle for a more meaningful beat
But his liability kept rearing its ugly head
Earlier in the week he growled at some people
He bared his fangs, they backed off
They came with complaints
But given the bad reception
They sheepishly left

He was reprimanded by his superiors
He was told to be more courteous
For which his freedom to function was curtailed
Those in the department ought to be exemplary
He was told in no uncertain terms

It darkened his future, his authority diluted
He was left to salvage his pride alone
He barked his frustrations across the divide
He could see his lot having to take orders

Where often times he had to work fast
His inability to stamp his independence
Was thwarted by not having the leeway
To act on his own initiative
His opinions were stifled
He was on leash all the time

A handler by his side
The life of a K9 police-dog

Prompt:
The given words - *darken badge liability*

Dreams

An extension of the imagination
Registers its presence in the nights
Not wanting to show its true colors
But rather flashes of staccato bites
Emerging for a split second or longer
Then disappears into Davy Jone's locker

Can one believe dreams that appear
foretelling of what's coming in the future
But why must the images emerge
And then wrecking, inflicting damage
Causing havoc in the minds of the lost
Playing tricks to test the human resolve!

A good dream is a bonus for good living
Bad dreams are the aftermath of bad intentions
Getting mixed up juxtaposed in lots of misgivings
Prodding the human self in torrid simulations

In classic fashion and in myriads of colors
In the realms of the subconscious

Tunnel of Love

It leaves one full of envy
Encroaching the tunnel of love all green
And with that strange air of mystery
Walls covered with moss and lichens

Tracks leading to hopes and visions
Of couples bent on joint success
Is forever open to aspiring innocents
Readying themselves to happily access

The life of a loving couple with all ramifications
Many will make it together sans difficulty
And the risks inherent in all permutations
But some few rudely discover a partner unworthy

That is life a blend of good and bad
Forever twirling the wheel of fortune
On pivots well balanced tacitly made
For two hearts to elucidate their eloquence

Prompt:
Picture prompt showing the entrance
of a tunnel with its sides colored green
covered with moss and lichens

Scenic Waterfall

It may be damaging
to the environment
I concede that
I'm on your side too!
But the same cannot
be said of everyone
Humankind are most unkind

I have been through a lot
And it had been a long time
My patience is fully tested
I have a legitimate right
to survive and to be heard

It is not an ego thing
You have got to believe me
I have to persist

We face obstacles all the way
Dams restrict our natural progress
Layers of hard rocks are no help
Yes, we turn ourselves into scenic waterfalls
But otherwise we are dead

We have not even touched on pollution
Waterways ought to be given their due respect
Is it too much to ask?

Prompt:
The given words - *damaging legitimate ego*

Stormy Encounter

His resolve was expected to weaken
into a hurricane of emotions
It could spawn in his heart tornadoes
of feel to cause flooding of tears of despair
outwardly seen as a storm surge
before it lost its strength

They were in effect leading to a
confrontation for a large section of his soul

He was in control however despite storm warnings
haggling for his love amid storm conditions
expected somewhere close to his insides
It was a resurgent of the area of disaster
within a clear-headed self in a day and a half.

Rains and winds swept northward into his head
Seeking refuge on the shelf of safety and
were not expected to lose steam

It closed the road to any redundant reconciliation
that yanked at sympathetic ears and the mind that
frequently were flooded with denial during
heavy uplifts of stormy encounters

Soaked unsparingly in part and skidding along
swirling waters damaging to his reputation
he reluctantly moved on!

Volcanic Eruption

The given words:
shimmering jet spewing thunder yards
page spill park rest steps curb status

Note: *The word 'spewing'*
gave the impression of lava
ash spurting out from a crater
The recent Pavlov volcano
eruption in the Aleutian
peninsula inspired this

A rumbling to life
was felt brewing
Across the northern
lights shimmering

An eruption plume was
seen in the distance
Jets of hot lava were
spewing in abundance
All spurting out from
a fiery hot crater
Accompanied then
with a thunderous roar
That well shook the
ground yards below
Where satellite images
showed a lava flow
Reminiscent from
a page in history
Of impending destruction
of previous many

Spilling out down
the northern side
Threateningly towards
a park astride
a small stream resting
in all innocence
Where at 15,000 feet
above sea level an ash plume
Hovering and steps taken
to alert pilots of hazardous
conditions in the area
to curb crazy maneuvers

Residents from afar observed
an incandescent glow so bright
With a dash of beautiful colors
at the summit during the night.

The long stretch of
heightened activity remained
On orange alert status
for many days thence

Monday, June 10, 2013

Secured

Rustlers were again on the prowl
Gone was his coveted prized cow
Left in the corral it was safe it seemed
Sadly in the morning it went missing

Won Mother of the Year blue ribbons
The envy of other settlers around

Could have fetched a little fortune
And life would have taken a good turn

His prized bull was luckily not taken
Safe and secured when it happened
It was in the farmhouse to be fattened
Blessed with the hand of Providence

He would have to start all over again
A process that takes quite some time
But now he must always remember
He could do it with a locked farm door

Prompt:
Picture prompt of a
locked farm door

Destination

A lineage traceable
To times long gone
Of the age when planet
Earth was the playground
Of creatures of gigantic
Size now extinct

A distant cousin of the era
Of the dinosaurs still persisting
To survive in modern times
An anachronism of history
Carrying the likes of similar
Looks of the fearsome

Others had changed, adapted
and carried the evolution process
through. Look at primates and
just see where are we now...

......so just where is your destination?

Prompt:
Picture prompt of
a huge iguana

The Sound Barrier

Image Deleted:
Image of Jets in formation

A crack of the whip and a noticeable sound
Is it a breaking of the sound barrier?

It is! A loop near the tip of the whip causes
the sound but not the tip of the whip though

In aerodynamics parlance this occurs when an object
moves from a transonic to a supersonic speed

Thus we have unwittingly been breaking the sound
barrier all along on stated occasions

But Yeager did it big time then with
his rocket powered plane over the Mojave
way back in 1947

Like the jets in formation
he did it with a thundering boom!

The Prince

Chuckles! I have reached this far
That is quite a long climb
But this pesky flower is in the way
Despite making it in record time

It is a pretty flower, a beauty indeed
But my desire is stunted I am left flustered
I must get across for I have a date to keep.
The evil is afflicting me hard and I'm all frustrated

I have been through a serrated existence
Time is fast moving and my chances in deep abyss
Fading by the minute the curse is an irritant
A flower between me and that all important kiss

Prompt:
Picture prompt of a frog on a tree branch
whose progress is blocked by a flower in
bloom along the branch

The given words:
chuckles evil serrated

Beauty in Danger

Image Deleted
Image of a train ploughing
through deep snow

Undulating terrain
Of pure white as far as the eyes could see
In the cool mist of the morning
Blanketing the countryside
But hardened on the tracks
Not burdened lately
By vibrations of the Iron Horse
Now menaced with abundance of snowfall
For the week that was
Of beauty in tranquility

A lone freight train
Ploughing through the snow-drift
Speeding and pitting its strength
Through slush and nature's goodness
A penchant to madness
Volatile in consequence
Imminent danger thrown to the wind
But still insisting on arriving in time
Of ferrying its weight
To reach its destination
Of beauty in responsibility

Risks taken against nature's rights
Testing man's prowess in his fight
Of wanting to keep to his schedule
Was it not beautiful?

Prompt:
Beauty is Everywhere

The Jazz Great!

Image Deleted
Image of Louis Armstrong with his magical trumpet

The given words are:
cut shattering splits crazy cave giggle chattering
moonshine load wake scoop anything sense

Man and his plaything
Have trumpet will travel
A cut above the rest
A legend in his time

A frog in his throat
The shattering boom of his voice
Splits the air, it was just crazy

Hello Dolly! Oh, Hello Dolly!

The roof caved in
And the giggle faintly audible
The chattering stopped
The moonshine boys took a breather
They stopped loading their barrels
in the wake of his mesmerizing tunes
A musical scoop, an extravaganza
Anything and everything

Sock it to them, Satchmo
They sensed a heavenly evening

Fireworks at Disney World

Image 1 Disney World's Magic Kingdom, Florida
Hank's loving wife, Shadah, daughter Azlin and
son Hafidz. Youngest son Azhar, still a tiny tot
then in the pram

A sudden boom momentarily, a quiet and darkness
Then the skies lighted up, an umbrella of colors engulfed the night
Just as sudden a few more followed sprinkling myriads of goodness
Evoking effects of noise, smoke, floating materials and light

Rocketed upwards flames and sparks of euphoria
Into the air to explode in variety of sizes, shapes and flavor
Accompanied with whoops of joy and shouts of hysteria
A family fare in all innocence to rally around together

Sophistication in fireworks management was not obscure
Aerial fireworks launched with compressed air rather than gunpowder
The display shell exploded in the air using an electronic timer
Put to good use in the Disney's Epcot night time spectacular

Image 2 Disney World's Epcot Center, Florida.
Hank's son Hafidz with Epcot's 'Golf Ball' in
the background

Compressed air launch was logical and a better alternative
Ensured greater accuracy in height and timing of activities
Disney the largest consumer of fireworks in US perspectives
The fireworks were used to accompany their many festivities

All well and good to be able to enjoy such offerings
Injuries and accidental fires occurred, even premature explosions
For both ground or aerial fireworks came with risks of sufferings
Remember the San Diego botched display that went up in 15 seconds!

Besides the noise what about environmental pollution
Potential health risks, hazardous by-products, debris and acid rain
We were still lucky fireworks were not done on a daily occurrence
Nor were fireworks factories accidentally obliterated and flattened!

Hustling

The others are now nicely paired off
Alone on dance night is not an option
Check! Adopt an approach that is soft
To win over a fair lady's attention

Unlucky for my regular date is not here
Just as well it's time now to put it to test
Have I lost my touch and how do I appear
What's best approach to test my prowess

Alone by any chance? *No! I'm with someone else*
Say, can I join you? *No! I'm not disintegrating*
Create sympathy appear deprived and helpless
You have a light? Yes! That's a classic opening!

Prompt:
Picture prompt of a man at a party
offering to light a cigarette to a lady

Needling the Conscience

The given words:
mess answers *tracks* gas edge
files lie *complex pale class still*

It was all in a mess
He was trying hard to reach for
answers at the scene of the crime

94

He stepped on the gas
He diligently traced his tracks at the
edge of the forest where it was most foul.
He was trying his best to garner evidences
relating to the files on the case

Not wanting to succumb to the lies
propagated by the body of people
siding with the witnesses he moved on

Complex in its make-up a pale
comparison to those in its class
but just as amazing he checked
on the hard facts

He tried to put forth assumptions
goading them on till blue in the face
Acceptance was still difficult to assail

Holding on to good principles
he hoped for the break-through to
wrap up the loose ends. He searched
himself till he could not anymore

He had to give way to his conscience!

Wednesday, June 26, 2013

A Face of Innocence

It's all about face
An image so sacred
A portrait of one
Where there are no takers
To others on earth

Even identical twins are different

In physical looks
A person is one and only
No two persons resemble another
How so unique
How so sublime

The wonder of nature
Providence has a hand
But let nature take its course
The individual
Is unto himself
It's his domain
It's him to savor
It's him to take cognizance
A look in the mirror

The portrait of a mother's pride
And no one to dispute!

Prompt:
About Face

Don't Play Mickey with me!

Was originally christened by Walt
as Mortimer Mouse
But his wife Lilian thought
Mickey was more appropriate
Following his visit however
to Warner Brothers studios
Mickey Rooney claimed
Walt had named it after him

Mickey Mouse was not alone
He had friends around
There's Minnie Mouse
his girlfriend
Pluto his dog Donald Duck and Goofy
And he was an official mascot
since 1955 of Disney

A runaway success Mickey
received nine Academy
nominations.

What's more on
his 50th anniversary
in 1978 he even had a star dedicated
to him at the Hollywood Walk of Fame
A life with cartoons is such a joy
and one with Mickey is so therapeutic
What if there was no Mickey
And there is no Disney
Youngsters will not be saying
'Don't play Mickey with me!'

Prompt:
It All Started with a Mouse

An Island Paradise

The given words:
bear bend fallen *bridge meadow heaven*
lane retreat bird rock unstable wild island

Bear in mind that
A bend of the road
Or a fallen bridge
May not be such
An obstacle

A meadow in heaven's
Likeness is a savior in a
Lane of peace a likely
Retreat from
Birds of prey

It may not rock the
Unstable nature of a
Wild imagination but
Can well be a catalyst

An island paradise
Is still within reach!

Life's Journey Well Taken

Triumphant in his bid
It's not so much the destination
It's how one comes through it
Journeys spice off all tractions

One is not totally bruised
Going through life's path
But one cannot expect to just cruise
Nonchalantly unscathed

Facing life's challenges
Subjecting one's resolve to test
May be hell in many instances
And relaying failures are hard to profess

But one laughs it off when all are done
Reflecting how very close it is driven
Mistakes are not material to spoiling all the fun
And eventually splashed across as forgiven

If some dividends are forthcoming
It's been life's risks worth taking

Being Cruel To a Baby!

How cruel it can be
How awful!
It was heavenly

A minute ago

It was snug
Floating and cushioned
At every knock
And now just jettisoned

What a shock!
A slap on the butt
The water is cold
You inconsiderate adult!

Ok, I'm now all wrapped up
Comfy and warm
This is it! Peace at last!
But I'm being ogled around
Hey! no pinching, ouchy!
Just you look
No monkeying around
Don't touch me!
Just leave me alone!

Prompt:
Birth

Misgivings of Mercantile Mayhem

Note: *To write on 'atmosphere' or mood. We are also
asked to state our mood. Hank's mood is one of concern
The apparent economic woes looming ahead not given its
due seriousness. Generous use of words starting with 'M'
to give effect to the mercantile approach and background*

With weird misgivings he plotted his next move
He needed to mollify his stance mundane as it was
Mitigating factors macabre and menacing in nature
Were not migrant in his choice but might malfunction

A motley of events midget in seriousness but maverick
In approach played a medley of musical interludes in
Mystical ways in his mind. A mishap of mayhem of sorts
A marathon of strains meandering and menacing

Minions of society manacled in their bids marooned
Into exclusivity wanting to be magnanimous to maintain
A semblance of mercantile preference muted in munificence
Maimed in their efforts in monotonous business pursuits

A malingerer wanting to meddle in matters of an entrepreneur
Making money in millions but have murky ideas of making it big
A modicum of honor though muted pushed misshapen efforts
To be a millionaire in thinking but minuscule for starters

Mindful of maverick economists who accurately predicted the
Sub-prime woes before and who now saw a bigger malfunction
Looming ahead chronicled in Aftershocks with misgivings not
Unfounded warning mortals of impending Depression ahead

Puzzling to Puzzled Minds

Puzzles are a fascination
an intellectual refuge to test
emotions so tickled

Puzzling to some
of how so engrossed

one gets in unraveling
a cross-word puzzle

Time and patience are impacted
frustrations ensued
solutions pursued
with shrapnels of ideas blasted into
brains that refuse to operate
and co-operate

On hindsight its sobering effect
is notably a savior to sustain semblance
of balance and
of logic and sanity

Mind games, memory exercises
puzzles, all impinge on the conscious
to bring out the best in the sub-conscious
to counter a debilitating memory loss
for which a cure is so elusive

Pathetic to observe brilliant minds
plunge so deeply in the dark abyss
of no return of the curse of dementia
a bane to the aging minds

God forbid!
Blogging helps!

Locked in or Locked Out

The given words:
trigger lock delinquent hapless birds

Locked out, an indication one is not wanted
The snow, rain and cold out there triggered
Hoping though the weather is kind
A respite in a way to give time
To reflect on what had transpired
For it wears off even the physically well structured

The vagaries of the elements
Impacting on the emotions
Running hot or cold
Subjecting the poor souls
To health constraints beyond
The being is tested and one suffers alone

Locked in is more dreaded
Behind bars or 'house arrested'
Confined within the four walls
With no personal freedom at all
Free movements are restricted
Or not at all accorded

Is it a good choice then
being locked out or locked in
Emotionally the effect is the same
Whether innocent or delinquent
Allowing those having the power
To allow the rat in the sewer
To act out their whims and fancies

To various forms of indignities
To which the hapless
Jail-birds and nameless
are subjected
to have their resolve restored

Desires in Calm Waters

Whispers of sweet nothings softly
Knocked a little a time expecting
How efficient it was to be silly
Pushed in as much of the same trying

Love knew no bounds but still insisting
Mindful of being snubbed as before
Trudged on tenacious in reckoning
Persisting and pulsating even more

A sly smile was all that he perceived
But just as well there was a response
Open your heart and not to deceive
Desires in calm waters not enjoined

A New Planet

The given words:
lab detect mistake leave friends together
translate conscience note rest second

The space lab was jubilant
It managed to detect a new planet
Make no mistake, it orbits its own sun
With a chic given name, Fomalhaut

Fomalhaut-b is the new planet named
Surrounding it a Saturn-like ring structure
Comprising brown and gold colors aflamed
Leaving them like friends close together

Translating a conscience long noted
Are yet to reveal from the rest of the galaxy
Likely second planets may still be discovered
Takes time it may seem but still very likely

Recycling Old Car Models

Myriads of colorful balloons
Lifting 'some baggage' up high
Old fashioned way to be air borne
Relentlessly reaching for the sky

Great imagination is necessary
To keep the baggage afloat
Such spells in defiance of gravity
Not too soon to gloat

Precursor of hot air bubbles
In big wicker baskets if one dares
Dreams come true in old car models
Driving in space is a daring fare

Prompt:
A picture prompt of an old car high in
the sky being lifted by many balloons

Melt-down, Pessimism Ahead?

A change for the able
A motivation no less
To catapult one to a higher level
Vying for one's best
Sensing a world of unlimited wants
But stifled by scarce resources
One at the forefront
Discounting unbridled losses

Searching for solutions
To overcome shrinking revenue
Conflicts abound with options
How to make out anew

The business world revolves
On its own momentum
Extending a reach to involve
The reckless shenanigans

But the economy is rudely facing
Trying times without recourse
A market smaller in offerings
Contracting on untimely remorse

Gets frightening
Just so thinking
How it had been

Remember the
previous sub-prime thing!

Prompt
The Future

Lethal War Machine

An anachronism
of the dinosaur period
Insisting in maintaining
its peculiar appearance
which had not changed
A crocodile a lethal
fighting machine

Bulky and unwieldy
Depended on stealth
In hunting for its booty

Its hunting grounds
Pools of water dark and murky
Priming itself just below the surface
Eyes nonchalantly darting
barely unseen

An unlucky calf
Stooped to take a drink
Jaws snapped
On soft thigh muscles

Rolled and whirled
In the water
It never stood a chance
Poor thing!

A Superhero of Old

My recollection of superheroes
Were mainly of the Big Three of that vintage
Superman, Batman and Robin and Captain Marvel
Of them Captain Marvel left most memories

The impact was on account of many reasons
Captain Marvel had the strength of Superman
He could fly and righting wrongs where he found
And more so his shout-out phrase 'Open Shazam'!

First to be featured in his own serials on film
Sadly it did not sustain its own 'immortality'
As a result of a copyright infringement suit
It went into oblivion

There were hopes of its return
But given the present crop
Of superheroes wannabes
With all sorts of electronic peculiarities
It would have to have more on its plate
To come back to its heyday
Of superiority!

Wonders of The Universe

The wonders of the Universe
Movements on its own momentum
An inertia driven witnessed
in light years from a distance
A clock-work precision

Sighted rings of dust!
Nicely inclined
Revolving every ten hours
Naked eyes could not
seek from afar for Jupiter
but with telescopic help

(Each stanza is of 140 characters)

Prompt:
To write a 140 character verse fashioned along
that of twitter postings

Greener Grass The Other Side

It's putting a face to the oft heard
saying of the grass is greener on
the other side

The cow thinks so too having
kneeled under the barbed wire

It's no more a metaphor
but literally proving the reality
and wisdom of the saying

Visually it is very apparent

That of envy and motivation to others
of the grass being greener
on a neighbor's turf

Prompt:
A picture prompt of cow trying
to slip under a barbed wire fence
to greener grass on the other side

Musical Sounds Unplugged

Just a minute all that it takes
And a change of instruments
To those who wanted to return to makes
That brought fun to their generation

Of music they were used to before
Of instruments not tainted by fashion
Just plain natural acoustics and more
Transmitting the string's vibrations

In a sound box to amplify the sound
At its own resonances and frequencies
Of the strings plucked with a plectrum
Of bygone days with all its melody

Before the advent of artificial interferences

In loud sound fare of electronics
Talents of a lone entertainer enhanced
The finesse of good music

Of bass guitar melody or rhythm
Unplugged and holding court
Of an awesome performance
All on his own accord

Seeing Double

The given words:
Breath sense sends shadow head bread
salt thread gravity landscape plans shoes

Seeing double
Seeing trouble
Is it for real?
No, it's not funny
With bated breath I sense the oddity
It sends a shadow of doubt in the head
What of today's bread!

It seems queer
Of what's on offer
No, not just surprised
Even thinking
and with a pinch of salt
It seems weird

Two of a kind
making copies
Of each other's hand

111

And in 3-D!

An entirely weird thread
The gravity of the situation
Knocks on an unsuspecting
A landscape of wonder!

Tell me what's the plans
No goody-two-shoes
Just the plans
Just tell me the plans
It'll be double the fun
Don't weigh in the dumps
It'll turn out to be a good run
If we play our cards well
It'll be swell!

Prompt:
Picture prompt of two hands
one with a pencil sketching an
exact replica of its imagein 3-D

The Fro-yo Re-emergence

The Fro-yo Re-emergence
Has a lot going for it
An USD one billion dollar industry
Fro-yo is here to stay

Puts class into a first-date treat
Exudes semblance in young hearts of romantics
Makes ice-cream look so ordinary
Compounded with being food so healthy

Frozen yogurt is taking over the world!
It comes with exotic names
And a wide selection of toppings
Targeting the young
and ardent weight watchers
Employing twitter and FB
To zero in easily to its locations

The re-emergence echoes
a previous boom
that started in the 1980s
It was hugely popular by the mid 1990s
But sometime later consumers declined,
and the product vanished without a sigh

But the re-emergence has a life of its own
Frozen yogurt shops have been springing up
throughout midtown and downtown Manhattan
This healthy trend finally made its way uptown
with Chill Berry in Harlem
And the same can be said of Berry Chill
which sought Chapter 11 protection
but is now bouncing back with its Culture
mobile trucks in Chicago district found
at many different locations

The big names of frozen yogurt chains
Yogurtland Menchies Red Mangoes
TCBY Pink Berry Orange Leaf among others
are all cashing in on the game

Prompt:
Chills

It's a Tuft War

Image Deleted
Two Geckos Locked in a
Fight to determine their Tufts

The given words:
berserk duplicate quibble

It's the way of the world
When there are two of a kind
It's a *duplicate* of sorts
It would be just fine

If they can find their own tufts
But as always the case
It's space and acting terse
Instinct determines the pace

Just a *quibble* and they erupt
They take positions aggressively
The equation is quick to disrupt
They bite lash and gnarled incessantly

They just go *berserk* without warning
Like the dog in the manger reacting
Not unlike a human provoked parrying
Off blows after blows contending

Each having as much rights
To wrench away at victory
Insisting to resolve to fight
To retain a semblance of authority

The Salar de Uyuni

Image Deleted
Collecting Salt at the Salar de Uyuni

The Salar de Uyuni in south-west Bolivia is currently the world's
largest salt flat at 10,582 sq km (4,086 sq mi). It is covered by a
few meters of salt crust.

The large area, clear skies and exceptional surface flatness
also make the Salar an ideal object for calibrating the altimeters
of Earth observation satellites - wiki

A cursory peek at a salt flat
a salt desert of immense expanse

None would have thought
it sustained properties and
of a location
benefiting the world
which otherwise would have
been left desolate and barren

What were they may be asked?

That it was a few meters covered
with salt crust to support the crave
of taste. Not just that. It was also for lithium
in the salt that brought in more money

Its exceptional flat surface
a unique advantage
The world's largest there was
The flatness of a large area and the

clear skies staked its place as an ideal
site for space observations

Such was the richness of a cool expanse
of wasteland
which did not come to waste
but benefiting mankind in unusual ways!

Cowboy Stories

The Bedaux Expedition was an attempt by eccentric French millionaire Charles
Eugène Bedaux to cross the British Columbia wilderness, while making a
movie. He was also testing Citroën half-tracks and generating publicity for
himself. He set off on this unusual and ill-conceived excursion accompanied by
more than a hundred people. Also along for the trip were several dozen Alberta
cowboys and a large film crew. The expedition started off at Edmonton,
Alberta on July 6, 1934 and their goal was to travel 1,500 miles (2,400 km) to
Telegraph Creek, British Columbia. Much of the trip would have to be made
through regions that were relatively uncharted and had no trail - wiki

Images Deleted
Image: The Alberta cowboys who were with the Bedaux Expedition
Image: Hank Williams and The Drifting Cowboys
Image: The Brokeback Cowboys all in twos

Cowboy stories ran the whole gamut
Of the hazardous the pain and the skill

Of roving able-bodied men who sought
The Wild West taking with them the zeal
Of rounding up, to brand and tame wild
steers across plains or in ranches giving
rise to likes of Hollywood fame of Cowboy

greats Gene Autry and Roy Rogers

When later came the makes of films Italian
In the likes of Clint Eastwood and Franco Nero
that gave a new life to blood spills and guns
Very unlike the rough ride of the Expedition
Bedaux that trekked through uncharted
terrains and the romances of love life in songs
of the Drifting Cowboys and Hank Williams

To the modern day tough and tumble
of such fascinating teams like the Dallas
Cowboys in posh and grand stadiums of
football complete with alluring cheerleaders
as a ploy until recently when liberal resurgence
made the manly able-bodied he-man surge
to a higher level where companions
by twos of Brokeback Cowboys emerged

Lonely Long Distance Runner

The given words:
*circle concrete illuminate race incentive striking
pounding hitch stark scatter strain striking wallow*

They would *circle* the *concrete* jungle
With the dogged aim of being able
To run en masse along a route designated
To grab honors befitting a distance runner
Illuminating a *race* at full throttle to the fore
Such was the *incentive striking* at the core

A *pounding* pace with no possibility of a *hitch*

But a guarded regular rhythm of a pitch
In *stark* contrast to a quick dash of a sprint
Leaving opponents *scatter*ed way behind

He remembered the *strain* of training
At high altitudes and of running
To maximize a waning stamina

Mark of a marathon runner
And he was not to *wallow* in self pity
But to strive for King and country

Tuesday, August 13, 2013

The Sound of Silence

A mind entangled with tumultuous yearnings
Searching furiously for its hidden beginnings
Silence hooked up in relentless pursuit
Searching furtively for the right mood

Suspiciously without a sound but groping
Surreptitiously in the dark to make its bidding
Because a vision was softly creeping
Seemed to be guardedly approaching

Slowly it advanced a shadowy apparition
Unfriendly in make up an unwelcomed intrusion
And whispered in the sound of silence
Loud decibels shrieked but not apparent

The wrath of musical talents pressing to perform
Wretched were those wanting to make it stagnant
Squirming backstage in resigned frustrations
Wondering to go ahead and plug the equipment

No, the apparition was the power that be
Dawned on the group, appeasing him was priority
It wouldn't pay messing around with the decision maker
A musical ensemble in abeyance waiting for an answer

What Could have Been.....!

The given words:
Distraught, Habitual, Regulate

Reflecting on what could have been
A feeling of a let-down tugged at his conscience
They were teenage sweethearts growing up together
She was like a sister emotionally attached to him
He was likewise a brother protective of her well-being
They were close to tying the knot even
Each whispering sweet nothings to cherish together

Why was it allowed to go along the path it did
He left for a little while and she did not wait
There was no word and things were left to chance

He was distraught upon seeing her now
It was a far cry from what he had wanted her to have
When in their moments of togetherness
Of emotional attraction a teenage couple
They had eloquently professed to sacrifice for each other
Nothing physical just plain and innocent
Of wanting to emulate those successful
Those who managed somehow to regulate their lives
Seeing material richness and riches and emotional salvation
Successfully binding on just love alone

119

It just wasn't fair, not fair at all
If only she had not been habitual
A handicap she imposed upon herself
It could have been blissful
It wrought a naked path of dire straits
Which he could not fathom
It was with a tinge of regret
That what they had lovingly talked about
Just fizzled out into nothingness
It was a pity, a real pity
It brought tears to his eyes!

Erotic Fan Dance

Sophistication for a lady
Served a purpose of elegance
A fan a functional accessory
Useful in certain situations

A fan dance commonly seen
In many cultures in the East
Of traditional dance sequence
As an accessory of modesty
To hide the lower part of the face
In a coy manner of pretense
Found credence in Spanish flamenco
Even in some instances

Nothing compared to traditional dances
commercialized and tainted with adaptations
where erotic movements were thrown in
Despite dancers were covered
but of seemingly nude illusions

By whatever little could be hidden
Behind a couple of ostrich feather fans
Such were the wonders of Sally Rand
Arrested even in the act of performance
Deemed to be lewd and outrageous
First performed in the years of the Depression
Found acceptance through the ages
Appeared on stage even into the 70's
And paradoxically an advocate of niceties

Note:
Sally Rand was a burlesque dancer and actress
most known for her ostrich feather fan dance
Her most famous appearance was at the 1933
Chicago World's Fair where she was arrested
four times in a single day during the fair. This
was due to perceived indecent exposure after
a fan dance performance

I Cried Out For Clyde

Upon my daughter Azlin's Commencement
she stayed on for a few months in the States
Clyde, a Scottish Fold came into her life

It shared the apartment with her other
house-mates. Azlin got attached to it and
didn't have the heart but to take
it back home.

At the airport Clyde in its cage was watery
in its eyes 'meowing' pleading to be released
Azlin was shedding tears unashamedly on

the couch next to it sadly thinking Clyde
would be alone in the cargo hold.

It went through quarantine for a few days
upon arrival. Again tears freely flowed
before Clyde was brought home to meet
with the rest of our family.

It was such a joy! Being a house-cat it set
in motion the routine for the household for
the few years following.

It would lay down at its own corner upon
layered 'beddings' or otherwise loitering
around the house, chasing and messing
with the pieces of strings or little rounded
objects that we bought. The fabric lounge
set was subject to frequent scratching before
Clyde got 'shooed' away every so often

Daily chores of scooping the 'balls' of
pee and poo from the 'sand' and replenishing
same, a refreshing bath occasionally when
ticks invaded the silky fur, rare visits to
the vet and even being left at the
Pets Hotel when the family went out of town
for a few days. Not forgetting buying the cat
food pellets and sand from the Pet Shop

This went on for a few years of pet bliss
until one day it suddenly went heavy on
both hind legs and was dragging itself about.

The vet confirmed besides old age there
were some complications of its colon and
lower parts of its tummy.

It so happened it was due for surgery
when most of the family members were
away in Alor Star about 500km up north.
My daughter was at the vet but was called
back to the office we were later told.

The surgery took place anyway and Clyde was
alone with strange people around him. Clyde
did not make it.. When the sad news was
conveyed *I cried out* as the rest of the family.

We had Clyde buried in a shallow grave at
the back-yard but the sadness and tears
lingered on for a few days. More so when it
seemed that prior to surgery when Clyde
did not get to see us it broke its little heart
The vet staff said this could have
hastened its demise. It seemed possible.

Animals have strange ways of knowing
if the family members were close by or not
It could have survived if we had been
there to give the moral support.

We felt terribly sorry we were not there
when Clyde needed us most!

Prompt:
I cried out

Warrior of the Jungle

The given words:
sullen distinct irrational

It is meant to be
One, regal in outlook
Determined to stamp
its authority on others
Sullen but with semblance
of leadership distinct
from irrational behavior

The outlook of one focused
On enhancing its progeny
In the face of tussles from
The younger generation

Survival of those favoured
With strength of staying
power to maintain its hold
on the harem and the pride
Unless and until toppled
by a pretender to all the
trappings and the perks
befitting of one respected
as that of a warrior
of the jungle!

Prompt:
A lion

It's All About Advertising

Time in its life that twirls
When a fish of a kind
In need of space to move
Determines its directions
To fulfil a need to secure
Some form of freedom

Does it help to test a form
To let it be known to the world
For want of a better way
Than to seek the kind help
Of a newspaper's sway
With their kind of spin and spat
So to speak a walking advert
But considering the situation
a phenomena a swimming insert
Is bandied about incessantly
For posterity

A 'sandwich carrier' likely it seems
That walks the pavements, a lone being
Through a dense underwater scene
That's how it is to be so keen
Now weaving between stumps
To adequately be seen not in the dumps
An underwater advertising!
Nothing serious just some
whimsical spinning!

A fishy story
For all to hear and see!

Prompt:
A picture prompt of an
underwater advertisement

bitter cries filtered through

The given words:
bitter cries filter enough train gusting
fierce south keep pieces springs out

bitter cries filtered through,
putting enough feelings of success
into his train of thoughts

the gusting winds carried the sounds
of fierce barking further south
clearly the deer and the doe were
surrounded within the clump of
bushes in the center

the hunters tried to keep pieces of
information that sprung out of the
crackling wireless set to a low volume
for it would be just a matter of time!

126

Being a Master Chef

The given words:
edgy believe fancy cryptic bang anticipate
serene drumbeat rapidly broken bite calypso
crickets thrust precipice master climb moon
pepper soufflé leverage carriage fearless

She felt a little edgy to believe the worst
Fancy a cryptic message bang on the table
It was delivered a while ago. Little did she
anticipate a serene morning to bring bad
tidings. It broke her little heart

Drumbeat of rapidly broken tunes bit into
her memory. A calypso of shrill cricket sound
permeated the air thrust upon the precipice
of life's concerns

She had yearnings of becoming a master
chef to climb and bid for the moon. It was
a calling peppered with designs of soufflé
entrees, salads and desserts to leverage
on Mom's specialties. This was the carriage
of conscience upon her shoulders borne
of a family tradition

Sadly it was not to be. If only she had
been able to surmount the first hurdle
it would have been plain sailing

She was determined to try again! Her
fearless nature took over the bidding

Having Fun with Slogans

Dell says *Get More out of Now*
Ford was *Built for the Road Ahead*
Take Me To The Hilton
take a bow
With *Intel Inside*

Connecting People is Nokia's concern
Oh Thank Heaven for 7-Eleven
The Company for Women, that's Avon
For women too
The Ultimate Driving Machine BMW

Relax, It's FedEx

At JC Penny
It's all Inside
I'm Lovin' It, that's McD
Nike says *Just Do It*

Landing a Big Catch

Big game hunting
By a puny little match
He did not think
He'll land a big catch
That's how life is
Luck is passing by
When least expected!

But be open
Putting in a bid
Is a simple operation
When saddled with good returns
One gets confounded

A good catch arising
May just be lying there
With no means of landing
Unless one needs to spend
To facilitate its journey
to shore

Good fortune is always
accompanied with testing times
Whether one can stomach the days
For Providence is a great Equalizer
One must be prepared!

Prompt:
Picture prompt of an angler
landing a big catch.

Unwittingly He got Entangled

The given words are:
hillside patches gathered ghost spill sharp
exact swamp unbidden worship where edges

The odds were stacked all against him
Trudging up the hillside amidst patches
He gathered his thoughts
Not a ghost of a chance

129

So he believed
The day seemed drab

Dark clouds were forming menacingly
It seemed peaceful but eerie
Not a soul in sight
Not a spill of a shadow
Couldn't this have been foretold
He was not sharp
A weak moment
Unwittingly he got entangled
Entrapped in a love triangle

A slight distraction all it had taken
Not an exact foreboding
Still a swarm over his thinking
Loss of someone dear
Unbidden to one's heart
One he had worshipped
But where is she?

Rough at the edges
He had lots to learn

Just So There's a Good Laugh!

A ladies' pastime snack
So they say
He said, she said
Lots of groundswell
Perhaps a little joke
Perhaps not
Juicy ones get better treatment

130

Building up an arsenal
Can be handy
To get the mortal flatfooted
Sometime later in the future

Healthy as a conversation piece
Unhealthy of negative consequences
Oddly enough though
Some jokes may not attract a response

Among men there are gossips too
But the underlying motive
Is more of having fun
Just so there's a good laugh

Of the mortal's sins
Which painted itself out
To be seen as plain silly
On how he should get himself
caught over an odd thing
A joke is a joke
There should not be any judgement
nor ulterior intentions
Just so there's a good laugh

Prompt:
To include the phrase -
Just so there's a good laugh

A Godfather's Natural Take

The given words:
conceal propose allege cement

He is quick to act
A Godfather's natural take
Will impose his will immediately
Let it be known

Don't mess around with me!

Not to conceal his odds
The underlings had better be careful
His purpose in life
Is to be all-powerful
Be it in strength
Or in finance

Work and perform with me!

Propose whatever to whet his ego
Hard hearted he's no fool
Refrain from small talk
Never to allege against anyone within
Lest he gets suspicious of one's agenda
If ever it comes to that
Then pick your choice
To be buried in cement
In a shallow grave
Or in a used oil-drum
It's morbid

I sense betrayal in seconds!

Hitting Hard on Punctuality

He failed once again
He did it once before
He was punished
He didn't seem to learn
Now he was back here

The angels were efficient
The moment it happened
And 'swish' he was transported here
That split second!

But why did he do it
He was supposed to be on time
He was here a second time
He had to do penance
He had to sit at the bench

The first time he had to sit for six days
For being one hour late
Now he had to sit for twelve days
For being two hours late

He had to be taught a lesson
He must learn to be punctual
This was how they were punished
Even for being late in heaven

The All-Important Announcement!

The given words:
hand swept flesh nest clever basket
blinked chance ripe secret stars

The great Egret couple
Dancing hand in hand
Emerging through a misty morning
From a rain swept night of cold showers
That tugged at the raw flesh
Heavy rain that threatened the security
Accorded by its nest of twigs interlacing
Brilliantly woven in intricate fashion
In a clever way in mystical conjecture
To welcome the next generation
of young egret chicks

In a basket of a fashionable home
Mother egret rubbed her eyes, blinked
By chance saw the reassuring presence
Of its head of the household
It was the ripe time she realized
to reveal the secret she harbored
alone for so long

With stars twinkling in her eyes
She declared proudly
Reliving that special moment
Of all mothers-to-be
'I'm pregnant'

Image Deleted:
A pair of egrets – a type of bird

134

It's Beyond Redemption!

Having seen the flower children
with 'flowers in their hair'. The 60's
were times of discoveries
It was respectable and acceptable
to dig the drugs scene then.

More so when musical's greats were
leading and lending a hand

The drug scene was the pull factor
Hendricks, Joplin guitar strumming
and belting great songs
Lennon with sleep-ins it was
all fun and games
Dr Timothy and LSD gave the 'license'
at the most opportune time

And the flower children?
They were lucky, yes, all were lucky

Why? weed and grass were
apparently mild! These were easily
made available. Snorting them were
considered respectable

Big money brought more daring variants
Acid, ice and what-have-you, made the scene
Expensive drugs, fashionable but lethal
Some were not even known
or readily available
but prescribed to Hollywood greats

We missed our idols
We missed Elvis, MJ and a host
of others who were knocked senseless

The game is still being played, the
drug scene is still very much alive

But the players are different.
Drug mules are tricked into carrying
them across borders.
Unlucky to be caught are languishing
in jails the world over either serving
life terms or awaiting execution

The end users found at dark alleys and
street corners in deathly stupor
It's no more just a fix. It's suicidal!

The drug barons on the contrary are
enjoying their ill-gotten gains
without as much of a conscience

The drug scene is beyond redemption!

What of a Trash Heap!

The given words:
daunting trash intensify fastidious

It was a daunting task
To determine what it could have been
Sieving through layers upon layers
Of trash of no known origin

It was not foolproof but rather
A next best alternative
To plainly extend guesswork
Humanly possible to intensify
Based on evidences relative
To other similar specimens
To reach some form of conclusion

It could reveal the social fabric
Covering food, clothing and implements
Which vowed to keep it a secret
Undisturbed for millions of years
Until archeologists arrived at the scene

The variety of artifacts could only have
Claims to prominence through conjecture
Of such scientific conclusions

Even the discovery of a single Java Man
Could still be mired in controversy
Whether it was an erect homo sapiens
Or just an ape or baboon of recent times

Being fastidious in collecting and collating
Of remnants of bones or skulls were by no
Means an accuracy of determining a fact
But rather of good methodology at best

Candor Not Asked For!

The given words:
faith manners brick cheat tentacles amalgam
slick vacant rage trash mouth gravel notices

Nothing prepared him for it
Had much faith in good manners
But it crashed like a brick wall
Everything went off balance

The cheat extending their tentacles
An amalgam of slick play-acting
and sweet talking conman juice

A vacant look often times were
the opening gambit before flying
into a rage unbecoming of one
given to trappings of high society

Trash from the mouth were plainly
dirty gravel extending notices of
the muck oozing with profanities

Attempts to fence in the emotions
came to nought and it taught him
a lesson - never ever bring back
home without prior checking a
talking parrot!

An Old Love Returns

Image: 1 Showing one hung up at the lobby where we had the launch

Been lingering in my system
Had tried to pin it all down
But it kept musing in my head
It was poignant, at times despair
More recently tugging at my conscience
Accompanied with a tinge of regret

What was there to do then
Something had got to give
Especially so on seeing
Some beautiful ones
Every now and then
In exciting colors

The opportunity came by
As sudden as the urge
It was a hectic two weeks
Tumbling head over heels
Over an old flame back
from the cold

Image: 2 My other love, golf

Feverishly I worked my heart out
Acquired a new set of primary colors
Dabbed them generously over the boards
Splashed here and there
Still not really sure of the outcome
But it was sweat and tears
I drew on what I had
For I had then an inspiration
All in acrylics

I managed 10 and hung them up
At my recent book launch

Something is now goading me
To work on my old love
More for the ensuing year

Deprived of Decent Living

The given words:
reveal greasy insidious glimmer
giant stature alive notion

It's a make believe world
Living in peril not wanting
But faces of despair in limbo
To reveal a scheme of things
Driven through a greasy tide
Of experience pulling through
A living more in tune with
Knowing of existing conflicts

Insidious in nature fronting as
Big business but hiding behind
Lawful outfits given to cheating
Whole communities of comforts
And shelter fundamental to
Survival with not a glimmer
Of hope than meeting basic
Needs of being and begging

Strong economies giant in nature
Swallowing minnows juxtaposed

141

Among many of equal stature
Basic in wanting to sustain
Some semblance of staying alive
But forced to put through a notion
That supporting a cause is better
Than desire to be alive and kicking

A Companion to Obesity

A monster of an offering
A Hillbilly Hotdog's 10 Pounder Burger
Gobble and munch no fearing
On the road to being an obese contender

Where to find it, needn't look far
It's a West Virginian specialty
Enjoyed by all and not a mar
to the state's 31% of adult obesity

The ingredients if one cares to know
Comprised bread, lettuce,10 pounds of beef
2 pounds of pickles, 3 onions, 3 tomatoes
And would you believe it, 25 slices of cheese

Fat content of 10 pounds of burger meat
is more than 800 grams of fat with ease
Or to put it more simply, it is the day's fats feed
For 12 women and not even counting the cheese

Hail all lovers of fast foods
The convenience that matter

Having it in a jiffy governs the mood
Couldn't trade for anything better

Prompt:
Fast foods

Gone With the Wind!

The given words:
depressed fuzzy sharp

Decidedly depressed
Could not hide his emotions
Others did not express
Any kinds of suggestions

What was he to do
It was a lone battle
Fuzzy and feeling blue
It was a big muddle

Love of his life
Had frittered away
His being nose-dived
Much to his dismay

Sharp in giving his all
Nurtured of good tidings
Felt rather small
All had gone with the wind

More guarded now
In expending feelings
Not way he did before
Which left him reeling

Misconstrued Insanity

Case of misconstrued insanity
Could he be faulted for a time
Lingering in throes of secrecy
Not really worth a dime

He searched his conscience
He thought he had it made
Sweetie Pie, he even gave a name
But she would rather have him dead

What did he do wrong
Whispering sweet nothings?
Choice of words all along
Not open to feigning

But he was not about to give up
Faint heart given a nudge
Plodding on would be smart
Time would be the judge

Ghoulish and Macabre

Uncanny designs devilish in nature
Its appearance ghoulish and macabre
Leaving imagination set to venture
Acceptable even without a lure

Transcending through time and space
Flirtatious roaming about the community
Scouring door to door moving in a maze
Trick or treats not entirely charity

But beware youngsters of present day danger
Times have changed now wrought with risks
Stalkers aplenty when opportunities appear
Defenseless revelers not given a miss

While among those friendly house owners
Once, one was known to have pulled a gun
Contending at the door a would-be robber
Or was it just a mere excuse of defense

Ghost-themed and morbid all so sincere
Halloween to fulfill an annual adventure
Having them indoors can be served better
To stifle probabilities of impending danger

"I'm The Greatest"

The given words
fists infinite emits distance hit precise
rhythm impulse invisible whisperings kneel

Fists flying, mouth spewing venom
An infinite fighting machine
Provocation emitted freely at its best
A handful could last the distance
Others did not know what hit them

Predicted when others kissed the mat
His predictions uncanny instances of accuracy
The precise rounds were quoted
When they would fall a crumbled mess
Rhythm of creations not on impulse
To them he appeared invisible
Despite loud whisperings of 'I'm the greatest'
Kneeling on bended knees the vanquished
His fights were remembered by names
Of those he defeated Chuvalo Cooper
Mildenberger Patterson Liston Foreman
Bugner Norton Tyson and a host of
other lesser known all because he
'floats like a butterfly and stings like a bee'

Prompt:
Muhammad Ali

What About the Letter

The given words:
befuddled breath whiskey mouth lanky race murky
marsh puddles pain razor silky isolate mouth

befuddled and perplexed
he remembered the letter
was still in his pocket, soiled
but he could not readily respond

his breath reeking cheap whiskey
mouth frothing and head turning
he could not expect to be at his best
how he regretted his boy's night out

a lanky guy he tried to race
through the murky marsh
but there were puddles to avoid
he was in pain from the razor sharp
old boughs rotting in the ground
only the silky handkerchief around
his neck sustained his resolve

he tried hard to isolate the hardships
and confusion from his clouded mind
he must make it through the slush
after all they cannot go on without him
he's lost but somehow he must make it

for tomorrow is his wedding day

Feeling Flighty with Flights

A flight into the unknown
The projected journey to Mars
A one way ticket to be gone
For spectacular space travelers

A flight of stairs is nearer to reality
Though replaced by escalators in many
Movements with one's own energy
Undoubtedly escalators make one lazy

A flight of four that is usual in golf
Play with buddies and lots of enjoyment
Lucrative sports, big money involved
For the golf pro with endorsements

A flight of fancy into realms of dreams
Fairy tales keeping youngsters in awe
But not with present day youngsters' whims
Where with computer games they get more

Prompt:
flights

Ode to the Eyes

Bewitching
Naughtily playful
Straining
wanting more
A pair that always looks good
Conveniently placed
In front
looking ahead
Not at the back of the head
Not Cyclops like either
but two dainty eyes
- doe-like
- glassy
- misty
- hazy
- squinting
- dreamy
- colored
- almond shaped
- slanting
- blinking
- closed
Though sometimes
sharp as spears
piercing
and can kill

But greatness
of Providence
for all those
a dual function

Eyes to see
Eyes for emotions
- Sadness
- Excitement
- Laughter
- Surprises
- Happiness
All bringing tears

But nothing beats
The come hither look
Bane to many
young hearts
And the stronger sex
who
pathetically succumbed
with just
one look

Prompt:
Writing the Neruda way

Toying with Abstracts

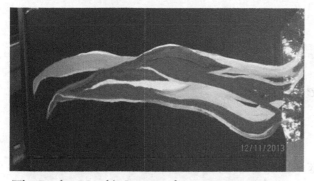

The Beak - Hank's Recent Abstract Painting

Note:
I have not been painting for sometime.
Recently I decided to try the present
generation of acrylics and paint some
abstracts. I just dabbled in red and blue
and came up with something like
the beak of some monstrous birds.

Taking on the bait
Of breaking off the shackles
Toying with colors and palette
How it's going to be handled

Not dabbled with acrylics
Not in mind of any targets
Decided to go through the basics
With a purchase of a new set

Try for hues of red of blood
Bright primary colors so true
Abstracts a choice to start
With generous splashes of blue

What comes of it now
Draw first and later decide
On the title that's normal
Is it a beak taking flight?

Sunday, November 24, 2013

Old Habits Die Hard

The given words:
habits create regard undoing suffering
virtue lessen gap however habits cycle

Old habits die hard
Scant attention given to discard
One can create due regard
But many do not act smart

Undoing of ingrained suffering
By virtue of gathering strength
Be rid of silliness long standing
To lessen the gap to reduced length

However breaking a habit
Is no mean easy but requires
Strong resolve to be effective
Once decided one never falters

Avoid cycle of tryouts
Stay true to a reformed self
Deserving then of a shout-out
Having triumphed above all else

Drifters Moving Along...

The misty Autumn morning
With hazy clouds across drifting
A drifter came into sight
Sheltering under thick blankets
Nonchalantly keeping pace so slow
Drifting in an even flow

Without a care in the world...

Leisurely gaining momentum
To forget life's many distractions
Slow inertia towards the estuary
Alone as drifters did in no hurry

Feelings shoved to the back burner
Not retaining some for any other
Letting life's troubles undisturbed
To garner some inspirations so absurd

She drifted along...

Just as drifters who walked into saloons
Without a bother they were left alone
They could have their drinks unchallenged
Quietly by themselves and off they went

Destination unknown.....

Prompt:
*Picture prompt of a lady under
thick blankets on a misty morning
drifting in a boat*

Ideal Peace On Earth

An adventure often withheld
Clambering in heavens shrouded
Likened to a gazelle ensnared
Across leaps of many white clouds

Peering down below wondering
Skipping through whims of fantasy
In guarded joys of blessed wailings
A pleasant surprise unlikely

Where are all the violence and fights
None are perceived no untoward signs
Conflict resolution questioning rights
To dispossess nations and all of mankind

Having their fortunes in their hands
Are bared as an open book to see
Wealth and expanse of good lands
Blessed with food for the needy

Chunks of greenbacks aplenty
Not grabbed nor fought but to hold
Thrown to the winds extravagantly
And no takers for the bags of gold

If only Paradise is staged unabashedly
On earth with such ideal settings
The world is a safe place to live in truly
Not to be but no end to hoping

Strength of Character

Image Deleted:
Madonna feeding her baby

The given words:
echo level listen means split spider pulverize
shuttle fly intact clear attend follow

To echo yet another prayer
Intent on a level of culture
To listen with the means of a
split-second strike

Reminiscent of a spider about
to pulverize its prey
an ingenuity to shuttle by
or fly intact with a slow movement
A clear strength of character

Madonna and a soup of milk
Affections to attend to their young
A reflection of survival

A vicious spider or motherly instinct
will necessarily follow a similar
pattern to feed young mouths

He was not Indispensable!

He ambled along trudging in guarded paces
His injured leg dragged slowly trailing behind
Created a light trail which quickly filled with water
The ground was soft it had rained hours before
They had unwittingly left him not realizing
He must have dozed off leaning behind the tree

There was no way anyone would come back for him
That would botch up the whole operation
They had taken great pains to keep it under wraps
Coming back for him would waste precious hours
He would have to make it on his own to catch up

Why he should be there in the first place
He reflected on the events of the previous week
They said there were riches some buried treasures
They were looking for able-bodied men to join in
He thought this was going to be easy money
He was behind in payments for his mounting bills
This was the easy way out he thought to himself
How he regretted it now as there seemed to be none
They had no qualms of leaving him behind
He had to fend for himself for the rest of the way

How was he so gullible but there was no turning back
He had only to be on guard to stay relevant and alive
He was beginning to lose his faith by the minute
Had to be alert his wits around him when he caught up

He now sadly realized
He was not indispensable
He felt he was being used
They might even decide
To bump him off!

Elegance of Being

The given words:
crisp exquisite magnificent

Crisp in a manner of speaking
Exquisite of charming substance
Magnificent in make-up of elegance
Can one be faulted?

For thinking of having intruded
Against the odds of discovery
Eyeing with eagerness the likes
Of maidens in all innocence

Wheres then it was ingenuity
Of the highest order to win a favor
Of a charming lady of leisure

But now with the preponderance
Of predators one is looked upon
As a pedophile on the sly
Can one be faulted?

Change For the Better!

Image Deleted:
Pink Crab Spider
(Changed color overnight upon shedding its skin)

Festivities were over been through almost
Few more days to the ensuing year
On reflection how luxuriant had it been?

New year resolutions that malfunctioned
Getting on in years slowly but surely

But nothing macabre maimed the thinking
Still writing and magnanimous in attitudes
Healthy but provocative in thoughts

Change! Wrench away on the brains!

(55 words)

Prompt:
To write a 55-word verse
on the theme 'change'

The Cowboy in Him

Image Deleted:
Bronco on the Open Range

He dug into his heels
The stirrups impacted deeper
The stallion lunged forward
It had been a long day
But he got his wish
Sitting pretty as cowboys would
The mount acted in unison
It transformed its pace
And progressed faster

How he loved to be back
On familiar territory
He questioned his wisdom though
Of trying to relive a page of his past

He was a lone cowboy
In the big country
He had his buddies then
And they roamed the plains

His fortunes took a turn for the better
A rich uncle upon his demise
Bequeathed large sums of wealth
And an ongoing outfit bearing the family name
That brought him to the Big Apple
Expecting him to dwell in high finance
To rescue and sustain the business
Of which he had no clue whatsoever

But he had to do it
The family honor was at stake
He tried to lead the team
There were initial sniggers
But he managed
The trick was to put his money
On a whiz-kid to run the show
But not to let his guard down
Keeping tabs every inch of the way

Now he is able to heave a sigh of relief
To spend the festive holidays on the ranch
Where he rightly belongs
And forget Wall Street for the moment

It Worked All the Time!

The given words:
blast chance map integral answer
synchronize tints tincture tip think
A blast from the past
By chance prompted him
To map out a strategy

An integral part
of the answer
Was in his ability
To synchronize
All of the visual tints
A tincture of hope
In life's offerings

A tip he held on dear to
Was to face up to problems
To nip them in the bud
Before they became
insurmountable

Softly about it
Think!
It worked all time!

A Treasured Black and White

A fulfillment of yearnings
Caught between the eyes
A gaze of wonder triggered
A feeling full of amazement
A moment in time laced with
Memories of days long gone

Unpretentious as a reindeer
careening across the sky
Just days before
Traversing the universe
With all the festivities

Now the lull before the storm
The quiet before all the
festivities started again

Recording more snapshots
Squinting behind the lens
To focus on things mundane

Undisturbed in the house
This was what he had captured
Many years ago
Of himself
In precious black and white

Tattered at the edges
There were not many of these anymore
Now treasured for posterity

Prompt:
Picture prompt of a black and
white old photo of himself

Part II

Haiku

Haiku is a Japanese form comprising 17 syllables of 3 lines. It has 5 syllables in the first line, 7 in the second line and 5 in the third line, a 5-7-5 syllable pattern. It has no plurals and is usually referred to as a haiku or a set of haiku

Happy Family

Enticing! The script
is perfect young ones learning
the ropes in oneness

Bonding couples rife
with true feelings pristine love
exudes sober thoughts

Careers established
Palatable family
We have been through this!

Prompt: *script*

Tulips

Image Deleted:
The Black Tulip

Dumas set the pace
Mysterious and elusive
A royal flower

Long posed a challenge
Rare find if you see one a
common color yet

A phenomena
rare of power and strength
Hail the Black Tulip

Note: The Black Tulip is a historical
novel written by Alexandre Dumas

Prompt: *tulips*

Wednesday, January 9, 2013

Instinct

Image Deleted:
A Bald Eagle

The given words:
focused vacant pair

166

Looking from above
It tried hard to stay focused
The young had risen

The day's feed was due
Pandemonium! Hunger
was a driving force

Vacant looks sustained
It should change for the better
Midday was ideal

Flapped its wings, it swooped
down. Pair of prey its target
A mother's instinct

Tuesday, January 15, 2013

Anger

A pull-back for one
Seeing someone contorted
seething with anger

Life is unworthy
if embers burning inside
enhanced skewed judgement

Good sense drives a hard
bargain. Malfunctioned thinking
points to disaster

Prompt: *embers*

Politicians

The circus in town
A spectacle just as much
but more amusing

Big business lobbied
Rent seeking money changed hands
Greedy clowns unmasked

Sans trapeze chairs flung
objects flew like animals
berserk running wild

Colorful ones caught
in scandals even cleaning
ladies were not spared

The game did not change
the world over. Only the
players were different

Prompt: *circus*

Dusk

Day is done. They troop
back to their homes wondering
What have I achieved?

168

Dusk transforms to a
darkened stupor to welcome
a night of conscience

They seek peace of night
with hopes they are blessed nearer
towards nirvana

Prompt: *dusk*

Danger

Image Deleted:
A similar kind of snake that we encountered
More greenish at the lighter colored parts of
their body. One of the most poisonous apparently

This was Hank's experience on a day of what
seemed like fun for a 15 year old on a small
island a long time ago. On hindsight it was
wrought with danger but it did not matter then

Such countless danger
Landed on island bold and
brave folly of youth

The slithering kind
Emerged from under the rocks
Threw stones killed some

Swam to untied boat
Snakes with vengeance might follow
but devoid of choice

To return to shore
Weather turned bad extreme risks
Without safety vest

Prompt: *danger*

Sweet Memories

Image: At Marine World, Vellajo, north of 'Frisco
My late mother-in-law together with Azlin my eldest
daughter and my son, Azhar.

Hank and family had gone over to Sacramento for Azlin's
Commencement Day (graduation) My late mother-in-law
saw snow for the first time at Reno and was absolutely thrilled.

Cute baby Azlin
snugly in her tender arms
cuddling on her lap

Protective of her
Shadah and I were lucky
Her mother helped out

As a young couple
we were inexperienced she
was the guiding light

Sadly she passed on
two weeks ago memories
sweetly linger on

Prompt: *Sweet Memories*

Heath

Process note: Not really knowing of how a
'heath' looks like, this verse has versions of
a similar kind of land in our part of the world
It's akin somewhat to light undergrowth where
we boys spent hours of fun when young

Nostalgic playground
Boyhood arena, stage for
countless excitements

Catapult in the
back pocket roaming the large
expanse of wasteland

Light undergrowth rich
with little creatures hiding
to be discovered

Heath a treasure trove
lined with childhood abundance
of fun and laughter

Prompt: *heath*

Rescue

A rescue mission
Dangerous and uncertain
Both parties at risk

Awaiting rescue
Those not knowing nor aware
of what transpired

With trepidation
Subdued while hoping heart beats
soared and wondering

Worst if no contacts
With hunger gnawing stricken
plight in disarray

Rescuers often
Rescued in botched missions but
noble in resolve

Prompt*: rescue*

Volcano

Volcano erupts
Spectacle that man observes
Nature playing tricks

Brilliant colors a
show of power and strength but
Hides an ugly side

Krakatoa Mount
Etna Pinatubo brought
Untold destruction

Reminder of ills
Ought to be corrected
for mankind had erred

Pride

Hold on to one's own
Arrogance comes alongside
pride in one self

Pride before a fall
Not a reason to quarrel
Humane in belief

Humility nudged
Being aware is being wise
A classic end all

Prompt: *pride*

Happiness

Image Deleted:
Frog 'Prince' Waiting for a Kiss

Stellar happiness
Joyful exuberance not
holding back a glance

Complacency rears
its ugly head confounding
joys of nostalgia

Decadence of feel
Decimating youthful thrust
Fabric of folly

The elderly quells
designs to cause mischief but
sentiments wobble

Sakura

Image Deleted:
Beautiful Cherry Blossoms

Precious Sakura
Beautiful cherry blossoms
Adorning the scene

Taiko drums leading
sakura music of spring
of colors and sounds

Songs of old since the
Meiji Restoration likes
of modern Japan

Prompt: *cherry blossoms*

Stork

Storks decidedly
assigned the obligation
of bringing babies

A tall order but
a responsibility
of necessities

Laborious job
Not for the faint-hearted but
wherefore the ladies?

Holland sojourn

Tulips and windmills
Of canals and maple trees
Den Haag and Centrum

Delft Blue and wooden
Clogs herring in onions
fries with or without?

Dining is bliss hot
pizza Indische rijsttafels
Chinese takeaways

Edam cheese galore
One or in separate bills?
Asterblieft and dag.....

Greed

More than pandering
to basic wants greed creates pangs
of evil psyche

Slick in nature sly
in tendencies profusion
of selfish actions

Stealth in strategies
Dark in yearnings slaughtering
and slashing routines

Friends and foes alike
Fair game without recourse for
ruse and trickery

Jealousy

Resentment and fear
Notions of rivalry and
Suspicions of threats

Negative feelings
distrust pent-up ill will
of others' assets

Facets of business
romance appearance career
subject to onslaught

Destructive outcome
Panacea of ethics lost
to fatal pretexts

Wisdom

Wisdom makes a man
Judicious in his make-up
inputs awaited

Commands respect for
contributions to the group
Quells bad attitudes

At times wisdom comes
too late refusal to be
involved damaging

Decision making
with leadership imposed can
well purge time wasters

Hope

Glimpse in the future
Faced with uncertainties
Hope for salvation

Slipshod assessment
Picture not clearly defined
Possession not known

Snared and snarled at a
displaced soul with society
at each other's throat

Rich against deprived
Check the forces and face up
There is a way out

Courage

Courage is often
equated to swashbuckling
style and recklessness

Pushed beyond limits
Needs stimulus to perform
Not quite rational

When it is all done
heroes are feted but how
quickly forgotten

Castle

Mysterious, massive
monstrous, lording on peasants,
a power unit

Secured with a moat,
buoyed by its own tax structure
Lord of the manor

Personal army
with arbitrary powers
completes the picture

Takes much of one's time
Building castles in the air,
just an illusion

Shielded

Overcast clouds surged
slave to widening movements
to provide cover

Diffused heat enhanced
relief of those sheltered with
quivering delight

Gathered in radiance
repugnant of shimmering
feel of annoyance

Wretched the feel of
letdown of those entrusted
who failed the paltry

Prompt: *shimmer-*

Caterpillar

Image Deleted:
The Eventual Butterfly that it becomes

Soft tissue wriggly
Spurned by the squeamish welcomed
food chain provider

Vibrant immersed in
myriads of colors unfazed
eventual winner

The ugly duckling
story repeated rebuffed
but hailed as beauty

Dolls Festival Day

Doll Festival Day
March 3 not a day longer
Lest pain of ill-luck

Hina Matsuri
Neatly arranged on platforms
Dolls on red carpets

Power to contain
evil spirits dolls displayed
of Heian court dressings

Universal by
nature dolls are soothingly
joyful and revered

Note: Girl's Festival or Hina Matsuri the
Japanese Doll Festival Day. It is celebrated
on Mar 03 and not a day longer which
otherwise might invoke bad luck

Usurai (thin ice)

Image Deleted:
Thin cicada wings

Kigo in early
spring. Usurai is clear thin
ice on cold spring nights

A cool lingering
phenomena thinly guised
of sparkling diamonds

Semigoori like
thin cicadas' wings. Shiny
lined network of art

Note: Kigo is the season's connection to haiku.
Usurai is thin clear ice that normally forms on
cold spring nights. It's also referred to as semigoori,
liken to clear cicada wings

City Park

A most welcomed sight
Expanse of water nestled
among greenery

Coolness exudes feel
of serenity wildlife
frolic in the sun

Unlike city folks
within a concrete jungle
and seemingly free

Warmth

Image Deleted:
The Grand Canyon from the
Desert View Watch Tower

A serene visual
Three layered blended within
pulsating colors

Mid-spring facade set
in motion feelings of awe
Ostensibly cool

Not so, one of the
Seven Wonders carved out by
the Colorado

Seventeen million
years snaking through Death Valley
ever eroding

Prompt: *The Grand Canyon*

Anaconda

Image Deleted:
A Green Anaconda

Green with envy seeing
one so big. It is one of
the longest big snakes

Olive green with black
blotches along its body
Reason it is 'green'

Frightening to hear
Can swallow humans whole just
not for the squeamish

'Anaconda' with
its three sequels created
that horror feeling

March seventeenth a
remembrance to snakes driven
out of Irish lands

Happy St Patrick's Day!

Note: Saint Patrick is associated with the
green color and most known for driving the
snakes out from Ireland. It is apparently true
there are no snakes in Ireland

Prompt: *To write with
all things green*

Aomugi

Image Deleted:
Rows of Green Barley

Enchanting rows
Soft green idyllic wholesome
and kind to the eyes

The morning dew stuck
like pearls of sparkling crystals
swaying in the breeze

Billed most nutritious
supplement cover against
nature's impending ills

Prompt: *Aomugi (green barley)*

Haru ta (Spring Paddy Fields)

Image Deleted:
Green Paddy Fields

Coolness of weather
Expanse of greenery of
nature undisturbed

By the late spring a
vigorous growth rate ensures
sturdy stalks stand tall

Staple food to those
In the East supporting large
population growth

Deft use of chopsticks
Cleverly held with fingers
for way of eating

Shunto (Spring Lanterns)

Image Deleted:
Decorative Multi-colored Lanterns

Spring lantern flickers
Swaying slightly in the breeze
On a lovingly warm night

The owl stood its ground
Wisely with a commanding
view of life below

A Japanese fare
Innocence of evening
Sipping light sake

Cherry Blossoms

A fleeting moment
to be savored. All good things
are not permanent

Waves of white herald
beauty in fragility
faithfully in time

Cherry blossoms white
Spectacle of joy fulfills
an annual yearning

The Pink Moon

It'll be full moon on Thursday night.
It's known as the Pink Full moon to herald Spring.
It's not really pink. It's just a name given to a full moon in April.
It'll coincide with a partial lunar eclipse in the afternoon.
That might render it pinkish.

Those in Europe are lucky as they are able to see the eclipse,
so also in some parts of Asia and Africa.
But it'll occur well before nightfall in the US.

Full moon in April
Is known as pink moon of Spring
Though not really pink

A phenomena
This time comes with an eclipse
A rare spectacle

Chocs

Chocs come in all kinds
Swiss Belgian Valentine in
all shapes and colors

Melts in your mouth not
your hands was old tag-line but
good marketing ploy

Often wonder how
simple cocoa tree supports
a whole industry

Strength

Awakening is
realization of what is
strong and what is weak

Lacking in strength
can be overcom but
not lack of resolve

It needs passion to
push and build the sheer make up
of Man under siege

Prompt: *awakening*

Damage Control

Riding high hoping
never the need to look back.
The future beckons

Doors opening wide
Opportunities galore
The sun shines brightly

Dirty play rears its
ugly head. Ambitions get
stunted. Wrong cards played

Grovelling in the
dark. Picking up the pieces
Familiar story

Adam and Eve

Note: Jabal ar Rahmah (Mount of Mercy) where
it was believed Adam and Eve were reunited after
their wanderings. Spinsters have been known to
pray there in the hope of being rewarded with a
man of their dreams.

Therein Adam and
Eve, Man and Woman destined
to create a lineage

Succumbed to the snake's
guiles, whence united at the
Jabal ar Rahmah

What would the outcome
be if bite of the apple
had not been taken

Humankind within
Heaven's gates still wallowing
in all luxuries?

Bridge

Of human failures
miseries and sufferings
that wrought pain to all

Of human conflicts
destruction of societies
built over the years

Bridging the divide
is a great challenge to test
the human resolve

The Weak

The given words:
vigilant justice helpless trample

Way of the world, not
vigilant enough the weak
grapples with problems

The scale of justice
Favors the rich who peddle
Influence and money

Where is the fairness
The deprived helplessly cast
aside and trampled

Friends

Fallen off with friends
Egged on with desire to
Reconcile again

Wiser and matured
Realized choice of true friends a
Never ending quest

Make friends with many
For among them are gems to
cultivate with love

Human Failures

The devil may care
Sworn since the dawn of times to
Lead humans astray

The devil in you
Succumb to base instincts on
its instigation

The angel in us
As elusive as diamonds
Dropping from the sky

Devils unchained and
Angels shackled are the cause
Of human failures

Frustrations

The joy of having
someone dear to share joy and
sorrow was profound

A shoulder to cry
on a pillar of strength that
extended support

But it came down with
a crash not expected to
be wretchedly dumped

Strong foundations just
floundered betrayal thumbed one
squarely on the face

Prompt: *betrayal*

Sumo

Male dominated
A sport steeped with traditions
in modern Japan

Towering above
other underlings weighing
some four hundred pounds

Stomping and pushing
Grappling the thick loin cloth
Hissing and heaving

A fight lasts seconds
but adrenalin flow rise
to its peak all night

Prompt: *tower*

The Moon

The owl pining for
the moon an aspiration
in futility

What inspires an
object of love so far off?
Image in the heart!

Best to compromise
Patience of a wanderer
rewarded in time

Judgement

Judgement is a stand
after analysis of
all evidences

But emotions can
cloud and color unbridled
judgement is it fair?

Can we take the word
of one who is human and
open to weakness?

With clear precedents
justice is infallible
Not too much to ask

The Young and Lively

A world of a time
Young and active, hello world
We are all ready

Own bodily strengths
scant worldly possessions with
resolve to succeed

We know our stuff
With just determination
and in sharing mode

Push the pioneering
spirit exalting the will
and aim high to win

Some little tryouts
For starters is not a crime
Just do it get on!

Prompt: *world*

Change

Face it change is a
constant inevitable
to all and sundry

Extending its reach
affecting living things and
the environment

Rejuvenating
enhanced efforts to get the
expected results
Remaining stagnant
is not an option for it
is then regressive

What of Julius

What does the future
foretell good fortune and one
that is elusive!

Or of bad omens
'beware of the ides of March'
Something sinister!

Or of Caesar's shock
'et tu brute!' tragedy
in front of his eyes

Prompt: *future*

Stoned

Image Deleted:
A man well dressed
sleeping on a bench

A bundle of heap
He laid still in a stupor
Oblivious of stares

Had one too many
Stoned after a boy's night out
He rested awhile

The bench was god-sent
The crowd milled around to them
he was a homeless

Prompt: *stone*

Mijikayo

Note: Mijikayo (short night) is about the
Summer Solstice (June 21st) the shortest
night ie the longest day of the year

Mijikayo warm
short night of summer taste of
the season's secret

Right from the word go
Short nights shrouded in trivia
Playful submission
Ticklish and wanting
Short nights create an urgency
Fulfillment jagged

A Feeding Bird

Image Deleted:
A Little bird feeding on a flowering
Corymbia with red flowers

Can one be faulted
Seeing blooms red in color
Can these draw the crowd?

Not anybody
But the will of survival
Prompts a little bird

And in so doing
Creates a classic pose for
an enthusiast

Of Moral Fiber

Of exemplary
moral fiber epitome
of honor for all

A guiding light in
pursuit of a good cause as
expected of Man

Sadly the same is
not true of those immoral
with shady dealings

Prompt: *moral*

Seeing Double

Pleasant experience
of seeing double persons
who appear alike

But two separate
individuals with their
idiosyncrasies

Twins share wonderful
times but are there silly fights
and disagreements?

Or share similar
pain love and emotions when
even far apart

Prompt: *twins*

Taue (Rice-planting)

Most widely consumed
Second highest to maize in
world-wide production

Maize meant for other
purposes but rice is for
human consumption

Culture and regions
spawn dishes, wines and
desserts of all kinds

Obesity is
serious concern though but rice
reigns as staple food

Hotaru (Firefly)

Winged beetles never
ending flickers fill the cool
sea-side swamp areas

Rare phenomena
Glowworm lavae becomes a
firefly as adult

Locally known as
kelip-kelip a night time
tourist attraction

A sly mating game
or to hoodwink a likely
unsuspecting prey?

Morning Glory

Creeper of a kind
Climbing tenaciously of
parasitic sway

Morning dew sprinkles
on purple charms faithfully
with brilliant sparkles

Not cultivated
But a survivor no less
Holding out its own

Hasu (Lotus)

Revered by billions
The National flower of
The sub-continent

Endearing regal
Beautiful ambiance serene
natural setting

All encompassing
Brand names places music a
popular icon

A Flower

Image Deleted:
Shoobu a Japanese iris

Breath-taking landscape
Stable of wonders in land
of the Rising Sun
Shoobu offerings
Tenacity to survive
on its own spirits
Japanese iris
Bright summer mornings exude
brilliance of colors

Chirpings of a Male Chaffinch

Image Deleted:
Male chaffinch whose
chirping grew louder

Darkness bids good-bye
The stillness of the evening
is slowly transformed

It comes as whispers
In tandem with increasing
lights it progresses

A sudden build up
Crescendo of chirping grew
louder in madness

Prompt: *crescendo*

Piercing Night Calls

Image Deleted:
A Cicada Leaving its Moult

That sacred moment
Melts the quiet of twilight
Sudden piercing highs

As suddenly it
turns melodious layered
lingering but firm

Oblivious of the
encroaching dark an eerie
ensemble beckons

Loudest insect cry
Mating game or distress call
All sounding the same

An orchestra for
the long haul throughout the night
Morbid in nature

Prompt - *cicada*

The Dusk in Rain

Fading shades of light
Darkened in the distance in
colors of brilliance

The dusk in light rain
advanced faster leaving the
birds chirping alone

The heavens engulfed
Shadowy signs of life made
a graceful exit
The horizon did
accept the setting sun to
retire the night

Right of Presence

Courageous nature
Tenacious in its desire
to stamp its presence

Fortitude challenged
Endured a temerity
of tainted justice

Resolved to right the
wrong tedious in its make-up
but it ventured on

Prompt: *fortitude*

Ravished Coconuts

Image: A young coconut bored through by a *tupai*, a squirrel

Source: Courtesy of Pakcik Hassan who extended the above image with permission. The fruit was from a tree in the compound of his house. The ravished fruit would eventually drop off in time

Note: Coconuts would be vulnerable to squirrels. They would jump on the coconut fronds from tree to tree and were known to attack whole bunches of the fruit. They would normally conduct repeat raids so long as there were still fruits on the trees.

Some farmers with guns would pick them off with shots
But it was just in vain as they survived somehow to
cause more damage.

It happened again
Surreptitiously savored
The young fruits plundered

Coconuts attract
marauding *tupai* that bore
through the husks and shells

Criminals can be
dusted for their fingerprints
What about squirrels?

They gnashed and gnawed through
Sharp teeth a mockery of
nature's protection

No such DNA
to pin-point the culprits. All
were guilty as charged

Prompt: *fingerprints*

Affections Most Transfixed

A fabric of life's
offerings accorded to
young lovers in heat

Affections may not
be physical emotions
are triggered off first

It takes a longer
path to be nurtured but held
on tenaciously

When it does it is
bliss with sizzling vibrations
lasting a lifetime

Prompt - *affection*

Talents Thrive Most Times

Hidden talents are
nature's best not restrictive
but most free to strike

It is a game that
people play knocking doors that
refuse to open

One loses out for
want of trying dubbed an
unlucky gesture

But creations have
ways of making an impact
Talents thrive most times

Birthday Bash at Age Three

Image 1: The Birthday Boy with sis Sarah Ayesha

Image 2: The Birthday Boy Ready to Blow the Candles, held lovingly by Mom

Image: 3 With cheeky sis Sarah Ayesha, cousins, Norman and Kimie

Remember Little Naqip? How he had everyone on tenterhooks
the day he was born. He turned 3 today and what a day!

His big day today
Naqip turned three and he has
his friends around him

Mom and Dad giving
a special treat, a birthday
bash at the Mall

How will he take it,
as the music is blaring
and guests keep coming

Curiosity?
No fear, he blew the candles
most confidently!

Nonsensical Nibblings

Stricken strategy
Sacrificed a winning streak
and stifled success

Rapport not rebuked
or rebuffed reconciled a
recluse's reluctance

Outright oversight
Obscured likely odious and
obnoxious ogre

Wrecked in bid to wrest
wisdom from the wayward he
wobbled in weird woes

Prompt: *sacrifice*

Companions at Hand

Ignites human cause
Extending life's hand earnest
in bids of friendship

Occasions merit
sincerity in wit and
like indiscretion

Devoid of feigned feuds
facades of conflicts all for
warmth of human touch

Prompt: *companions*

Measure of Strength

A measure of strength
Design of character laced
with regal bearing

Reminiscent of tussles
for power typifying
kings of yesteryears

Pompous appearance

on the podium of honor
befitting stature

Prompt - *measure*

Trials and Tribulation

Still wondering of
trials and tribulations of
what life has in store

One reflects on why
it runs smoothly for some but
not for some others

Blessed those chosen few
Providence is always a
fair Equalizer

Prompt: tribulation

Mood Swings Malady

Privately one thinks
Upon realization mood
swings evoke some thoughts

Fluctuates from laughter
to tantrums within seconds

All without conscience

Mystifying to
the unaccustomed dreaded
by those familiar

Desert Pit Stop

Caravanserai
Fitting pit stop for weary
desert travelers

Head splitting stomach
churning rest awhile a long
tiring ride ahead

Tension eased music
food peaceful night sky locked in
heaven's warm luster

Note: Caravanserai is resting
place in the desert

The Kagura Dance Moves

Slow and guarded but
given to sudden bursts of
movements to music

Arms raised in slow dance
moves dressed in preponderance
of whites and flowing

Graceful elegance
until the devil came by
with boisterous make

Bean throwing to help
appease the devil also
a sketch at the end

Note: Kagura is a Japanese dance form
traditonally dressed mostly in whites

A Water Baby

A water baby
Prowess in water was of
utmost importance

Thrown to the deep end
Was no bother after all
for a keen swimmer

Penchant for water
Frolicking at the pool-side
was her kind of fun

Beauty of a Sunset

Beauty of sacred red
Wonder captured on scenic
canvas of skyline

Tempered glare peace and
quiet subdued in nature's
nights of good living

Crimson night red hot
Conjures raucous actions found
of Eastern specials

Brilliance of Ancient Times

Image Deleted:
Kama Sutra Preserved For Eternity

Ancient voices with
Lingering sita music
Sensuously flavored

Gyrating movements
Radiance of Kama Sutra
Rhapsodies of times

Tugged at one's conscience
To let ancient brilliance
Subverted blindly

Prompt: *Ancient Voices*

Separation Without a Word

Across ocean blue
Pining for you when you break
up without a word

Roving blue waters
come in between like slow drift
of huge land masses

Only memories
sustain good times of young hearts'
purest endearment

Note: This has to do with the separation
of continents from a big land mass

Prompt - *ocean*

Joys and Laughter at Gramps

Morning of clear skies
Torrents of laughter spilled from
joys of innocence

Splendor of the young
Family get- together

At grandpa's abode

Outrageous antics
Sauntering and scampering
Young and old alike

Friends were brought along
Greater participation
All had a good time

Prompt: *Morning of Celebration*

A Star Blue Sapphire

Precious stones beauty
enhanced in vividness shades
and various colors

Accentuated
Star of India is largest
known blue sapphire

Prompt - *sapphire*

Silent but Vibrant

Life's rhythm in light
regular beats assurance
of precious presence

Silent heart exudes
inner feelings of love grasped
tightly undaunted

Palpitating throbs
soothed pagan yearnings to prop
vibrant calls of faith

Prompt: *the silent heart*

Luscious Lips

Luscious lusty lips
Bewitching twitching puckered
wet and flaming red

Glossy lips shining
moisturizing of subtle
Max Factor colors

Louisville Lips giving
tips when they should fall very
accurate in all

Note: Louisville Lips refers to Muhammad Ali
who accurately predicted at which round his
opponent would fall

Prompt - *lips*

Elusive Inner Peace

Spreading an inner
feel unwittingly prodding
an undisturbed mind

Searching for truth as
peace within rare as shooting
stars on starless nights

Unsettled bubbling
breaking tranquility with
staccato outbursts

Unwind slowly to
voices of reason lurking
deep for salvation

Prompt: *peace within*

Risshuu and Beautiful Japanese Moon

Risshuu shedding off
leaves but full of colors with
Japan's moon yonder

Liken to life's fling
to maturity before
old age feel beckons

Melancholic stroll to
cold spell but signals start of
new activities

Back to School, sports and
Halloween, a plate full of
promotions galore

Prompt: *Risshuu (coming of autumn)*

The Guardian Angel

Beacon of honor
Leading light against demons
who lead one astray

Secure and safe when
subjected to temptations
of ways of the world

Provides guiding light
to all and sundry sadly
some will miss the boat

Note: The Guardian Angel is
also a pop group on YouTube

Prompt - *guardian*

Rain in September

Rain in September
Trudging through floods a will to
survive and move on

Excruciating
Vagaries of the weather
Testing feeble souls

Human resolve, a
veneer so thin but of strength
beyond endurance

A Shepherd's Lot

Dramatic change in
shepherd's lot. No more lonely
hours all alone

Now working on big
farms as workers or lucky
ones as rich farmers

No more shepherd's pie
Little Bo-Peeps or 'cry wolf'
out in the open

The Will was Absent

Olive branch secured
between its beaks it flew past
Subtly a message

Extended countless
times. A bother no less but
none who cared to see

Could they be faulted
For not giving peace a chance
The will was absent!

Prompt: *dove*

Orchids - A Gift of Beauty

Humble beginnings
Jungle flower hidden right
among green foliage

Beauty seemingly
Creation of a classic
specimen of love

Love and affections
Aptly an epitome of
human perfection

It held its own strength
Given names of royalty
the rich and famous

Wase - Early Rice

Sunshine bright above
Innocence of wild sparrows
Eyeing early rice

Abundance to share
Staple food of human kind
Birds have first option

Scare-crow empowered
Padi stalks in danger zone
Locusts undeterred

Prompt: *early rice*

Rivers - Laughter and Tears

Image Deleted:
Free Flowing Ganga River at Rishikesh.
Abundance of rituals and spiritual cleansings within its waters

Commercial life blood
Nucleus of activities
Dotted along side

Romantics around
leisurely flow of peaceful
serene surroundings

Beware a monster
Destruction when awakened
Lethal, lots of tears

Note: Monster refers to floods

Prompt: *river*

Wonder of the Rainbow

Note: Rainbows are created when the sun shines onto droplets of moisture in the earth's atmosphere. The rainbow colors range from red (on the outside) and violet (on the inside). Rainbow occurs when part of the sky is still cloudy and the observer is at a spot with clear sky in the direction of the sun

Red at the extreme
Violet at the opposite
Colors in between

Wonder of nature
Consistent in its make-up
Emblazoned up high

Coolness of drizzle
Persistence in appearance
Hugging Sun's rays tight

What of The Eclipse

It's either a solar eclipse, when the Moon's shadow crosses the
Earth's surface, or a lunar eclipse, when the Moon moves into
the Earth's shadow - Wiki

In ancient times it was believed a dragon was about to swallow the
Moon and the villagers would beat gongs to scare the dragon away

In modern times dark exposed negatives were used to view the
spectacular event. Dark sunglasses were not protection enough

Solar or lunar
In both instances the moon
came by into play

Gobbled by dragons?
Averted with din of gongs
Earthlings did their part

Exposed negatives
better than sunglasses or
even telescopes

Prompt: *eclipse*

An Eclipse to Outshine

Tries hard to impose
Hidden in shadowy form

The sun bids its place

An eclipse takes form
Envelops half the world to
submission meekly

What of Vision Quest

Vision quest: A period of spiritual seeking often undertaken as a puberty rite.
It typically involves isolation fasting and the inducement of a trance state in
a forest environment. It's for the purpose of attaining guidance or knowledge
from supernatural forces - Wiki

What of vision quest
Initiation ritual
From child to adult

Spiritual nature
Energies of creation
Guiding life's purpose

Test of adulthood
Through chasms of discoveries
Shadowed by elders

Prompt: *vision quest*

The Privilege of Older Men

As both saw palmetto and pumpkin seed extracts benefit prostate health, taking these at the same time may provide synergistic effects. Men who took a combination of saw palmetto and pumpkin seed extracts experienced significant positive effects with no adverse side effects.

But more recent studies however found that saw palmetto was no better at alleviating the symptoms than taking a placebo pill - Wiki

Suffers in silence
Privilege of older men
An enlarged prostate

Relief in combined
saw palmetto and pumpkin
seed herbal extract

But recent studies
on saw palmetto alone
not encouraging

Perhaps the pumpkin
seed element saves the day
all these while.. may be

Strangers in the Night

Image Deleted:
President Reagen awarding the Medal of Freedom to Frank Sinatra

The song was made famous in 1966 by Frank Sinatra. It was the title song for Sinatra's 1966 album *Strangers in the Night*, which became his most commercially successful album. The song also reached number one on the UK Singles Chart.

Sinatra's recording won him the Grammy Award for Best Male Pop Vocal Performance and the Grammy Award for Record of the Year. It also won a Grammy Award for Best Arrangement Accompanying a Vocalist or Instrumentalist for Ernie Freeman at the Grammy Awards of 1967 - Wiki

Of such a wonder
Of Sinatra and his song
Of unmatched talents

Of nostalgic strains
Of strong bidding for the top
Grabbed honors all round

Monday, October 14, 2013

Behind the Mean Look

Image Deleted:
Image of a fierce-looking dog
from behind a fence

It is looking out
The mean look gets one jumpy
This is fair warning

Takes to turf with
wrestling freestyle and tossing
Better take notice

Lurks behind the fence
Be careful with play-acting
Known to jump over

Blessings from Heavens

Image Deleted:
Lighted lanterns floating in the air
to show the way for the spirits to
visit those still living

Endearing spirits
Of loved ones basking in lights
Of blissful Heavens

Returning visits
To those living with blessings
For goodness in life

Lighted lanterns show
path back to Heaven's gates
to return later

Privileged few who
remember their ancestors
can expect visits

Spur of the Moment

The given words:
release spark enduring

Spur of the moment
Release of a spark varied
in circumstances

Dare graze the front of
the speedster's bumper a road
bully is transformed

Enduring moments
of ecstasy but next a
monster suddenly

Crying for a fix
Wayward son swiped the meager
earnings of poor dad

Fight Back Against Bullies

Fenced in idle thoughts
Yearning to be free but lo!
Forcibly held back

Languishing alone
Tiny room a make-belief
domain but not quite

Invoked tsunami
Forced running battle against
the likes of bullies

Fight back a signal
not to harass, only then
they learned to respect

A Book Launch and Poetry Reading

Image: 1 Hank's long-time friend OP Tan Sri Aziz
who read a poem 'The River'. In the background
are copies of books '100 National Heroes'
written by OP Tan Sri Aziz himself

Image: 2 Not to be outdone Hank's grand-child
Nabil confidently at the mike reading 'The Eagle'

The Haiku
Book Launch and poetry
reading done with great support
from family and friends

The Prose
A Book Launch was done for Hank's book *'Rainbow, Poetry and Prose'* last weekend Nov 10 at the Royal Lake Club. A modest crowd of family and friends mainly from Hank's old boy's network (from the Royal Military College) totaling 80 persons or so in number were there.

The Book Launch was performed by our association's President, eminent scientist Tan Sri Dr Salleh Mohd Nor. Hank is proud to mention here that we also had poetry reading by eminent poet, story-teller and blogger the wonderful Ninotaziz.

Blogger Pakcik Hassan from Trengganu was instrumental in getting Hank into poetry and Madam Ninot was the guiding light. Pakcik had earlier apologized for not being able to come.

There was also a poetry reading by Hank's long-time friend Tan Sri Abdul Aziz Abdul Rahman and by Hank's grandchild little Nabil who was just 8 years old (and he did it like a pro)

Hank wished to thank all those who were present for all their support that afternoon. All in all it had been an experience, a wonderful experience.

Thank you all!

Monday, December 2, 2013

An Energy Flow

Bent on a journey
To experience Qi by way
of the Waitankung

Peaceful exercise
Breathing control stimulates
good energy flow

Qi flows smoothly with
improved blood circulation
and relaxed muscles

Note: Qi is the energy flow stimulated
through a number of physical exercises

Prompt:
Qi (pronounced Chi)

A Beautiful Dream

Bedlam of madness
Illusions of a sane night
Wrought with nature's ills

Come peace and quiet
Medley of good images
begins to make sense

Beautiful dreams in
meager forms now taking shape
Blessed the chosen ones

Contrast in Nature

Through light and darkness
One seeks solace of purpose
Bidding all are well

Putrid and freshness
One maintains sanity to
Shackle exposure

Enjoy or detest
One is goaded to persist
In all innocence

Prompt:
light and darkness

Unsure and Unfaltering

Footprints in the sand
Sadly leading to nowhere
Unfathomable

Sitting begrudging
a better alternative
Undemonstrative

Seagulls up circling
Eyeing targets down below
Unmitigated

Prompt:
footprints in the sand

The Sacred Earth

Paradise on earth?
No comparison but a
human sanctuary

Greed and self interests
To meet human wants had forced
earth into conflicts

Law of the jungle
in tempered form remains to
give semblance of peace

Ashes to Ashes

Rising from ashes
Purple hues sneak from the dead
A new life reborn

Bird of a kind yet
again extending a long
reach beyond borders

Note: The bird phoenix was known
to have risen from the ashes

Prompt:
ashes

Dreamy Dreams

Image Deleted:
Dreamy Eyes

Woke up from a dream
Treading softly on thin air
A bed of roses

Some unfortunates
Wake up in cold sweat deprived
of such luxury

Trick is to be nice
Mindful on retiring
with good intentions

Alvae - a Forest Tribe

Lost in innocence
Not expected to save the
world but surviving

Given to tests of
strength meted on tribes who showed
resolve of purpose

236

Rally around their
leader to mark not just a
presence but a pride

Note: The Alvae is a forest tribe in a
fantasy novel by Adrian von Zieglar

Saturday, December 21, 2013

Expectations Abound

Image Deleted:
Puddles on the Pavement

Upon reflection
Of puddles on the pavement
A mirror image

Kaleidoscopic
Reminiscent of what had
been and what would be

Incoherent but
Expectations abound as
blessed as a new-born

Monday, December 23, 2013

Movements in the Desert

Caravans headed
towards blooms of paradise
With joys of music

Desert oasis
Extending hand to precious
life with challenges

Survival assured
Fabric of activity
Amidst searing heat

Prompt:
desert

Up the Ante

Caught by the call to
improve image and nurture
success for glory

Credible restraints
Magnanimous in actions
Graceful in honor

Reaping benefits
Jockeying for positions
Go! up the ante

Prompt:
nurture

Gift of Good Health

Gift of a lifetime
Savor the good life healthy
in body and mind

Pray to Providence
Extend a climate of love
To all and sundry

Peaceful devoid of
natural calamities
without blood and tears

Blessed with a good year
Accomplished with fine results
Better yet next year

Circle of life

Comes the time nature's
swing moods clamoring towards
beauty of spring-time

Riding high buoyant
circle of life about to
accord fresh upsurge

Steadfast in splendor
Greenery and flowers rule

Drab cold forgotten

Note: Looking forward to the beauty
and greenery of spring and to leave
behind the cold winter is the feeling
at end of December

Cry Long Forgotten

Forlornly an orange
sunset reclining atop
the high mountain range

A Tibetan cry
Yearnings for freedom of thought
Gift of expression

Submissive but strength
of purpose belies will to
survive undisturbed

Prompt:
Monks

Softly music treads...

Swaying in the breeze
Soothing to the savage breast
Softly music treads

Up over the cliffs
Unrelenting in pursuit
Penchant for the ears

Celtic endeavors
Rounding up of enthusiasts
Over the waters

Prompt:
Picture of sea-side cliffs

Tenacity of Wild Flowers

Dancing in the winds
Provocatively bidding
Of youthful vigor

Of varied colors
Ubiquitously bathing
The wild countryside

Squirming sheepishly
Upon nightfall and slowly
shriveled in the cold

Assuming vigil
in the morning unflinching
innocence of youth

Prompt:
youthful vigor

A Wish List

Great Expectations!
What the dickens, what is the
wish for the New Year?

Abundance of food
for the world's hunger and no
more missing children

Mankind is pleading
to search the conscience and no
more drones incursions

Finality of
the elusive peace and no
more calamities

Prompt:
expectations

'Cracked Pot' Resolutions

Tedious close to a
troubled year where many
gave sighs of relief

Radiance of new dawn
Heralds discourse of hope
Amidst trying times

Groggy hysteria
Conflicts and social woes still
casting long shadows

Resolutions that
meet part of intentions are
still deemed successful

Note: A cracked pot of water carried a distance
arriving half full was still better. Half of resolutions
met was better than no resolutions

Prompt:
New Year resolutions

Part III

Micro Fiction

A Micro Fiction is a verse of not exceeding 140 characters. It is more or less similar to a twitter message. A character is either a letter, a punctuation mark or a space

Cheer Up!

Image Deleted:
A teddy bear and a rag
doll sitting on a couch

Just you and me
Keeping each other company
No fun in being neglected
But let us not be sad or dejected
Cheer up!
At least no one whacked us

(140 characters)

Prompt:
To write a Micro Fiction based on
the image and to include the word - *whacked*

Two Hearts

Image Deleted:
A smiling couple and both
were sporting big eye-glasses

Laundering her smile
so lavishly
Happy today!
Yes I am
Your goggles so sweet

So are yours
Two hearts together
and everything that's nice

(139 characters)

Prompt:
To write a Micro Fiction based on
the image and to include the word - *launder*

Piggy-back

Image Deleted:
An accident where a VW Beetle
landed on top of the other car

A beetle might appear
small but it is no way
to overtake like so

To vie for first place
must still be subject
to the rules of the game

(140 characters)

Prompt:
To write a Micro Fiction based on
the image and to include the word - *vie*.

Whassup pussy-cat?

Image Deleted:
A Pussy cat

Whassup pussy-cat?
You appear lost!
You are all alone very
unlike a gadabout cat
Where are your other friends?
They ought to be with you!

(140 characters)

Prompt:
To write a Micro Fiction based on
the image and to include the word - *godabout*

Tabby

Image Deleted:
A cat looking at what appeared to
be a two-headed fish in a fish bowl

Tabby was fascinated
It was now a daily ritual
Looking intently at the fish-bowl
it just could not believe its eyes

What?
Two-headed fish!

(139 characters)

Prompt:
To write a Micro Fiction based on
the image and to include the word - *ritual*

Micro Fiction - Sunflower

Image Deleted:
A sunflower wearing sunglasses

We follow the movement
of the sun all day. I sport
sunglasses on the hub of my
nose for style and protection
So, anyone here to object?

(139 Characters)

Prompt:
To write a Micro Fiction based on
the image and to include the word - *hub*

A Maid's Concern

Image Deleted:
A maid rushing out to the car
with a purse in her hands

Madam left her purse and she
was going shopping!
She would not be happy without her card
Numbed with fear the maid
rushed out just in time.

(140 characters)

Prompt:
To write a Micro Fiction based on
the image and to include the word - *numb*

To Meet Her Craving

Image Deleted:
A woman walking in heavy rain
in front of a row of food-stalls

Determined to get her
favorite food she elected
to trudge in the downpour
looking for the familiar
stall which was not
at its usual spot

251

(140 characters)

Prompt:
To write a Micro Fiction based on the
image and to include the word - *elect*

Fun and Games

Image Deleted:
The wooden side-walk
in front of Atlantic City

Atlantic City of old
where leisure and pleasure
were woven into a fine
fabric of life's fun and
games to cater for all tastes
and types

(140 characters)

Note: Known for casino gambling
conventions and leisure.
Discover everything to do in Atlantic
City whatever your pleasure!

Prompt:
To a write a Micro Fiction based on the
image and to include the word - *woven*

King of the Jungle

Image Deleted:
A picture grab of a film crew filming a
live lion in the studio in an old black
and white film

A no-frills better off
with a fake lion that costs less
But we need reality
Might throw in a live actress
to put some color to the movie

(140 characters)

Note: Some play of words here
1. a) throw in a live actress – to include
   an actress in the scene
   b) put some color – a play on the
   black and white movie

2. It seems another interpretation is
   'to throw in a lady' to a live lion and
   turn it gory (which was not what
   was meant)

Prompt:
To write a Micro Fiction based on the
image and to include the word - *frills*

Water Babies at Play

Image Deleted:
Some infants jumping into the pool

Zipped off the blocks unscathed
Air-borne like a pro unlatched
Confidently in all fun
Cool dip in the summer sun
Such a water baby to match!

(140 characters)

Note: An offering of a Micro Fiction
and a limerick simultaneously

Prompt:
To write a Micro Fiction based on the
image and to include the word - *zip*

A Traffic Crawl (MF)

Image Deleted:
A man looking at the traffic
crawl going down the road

Annual jeopardy for HK folks
Traffic crawl out of the city

to be home in time for Chinese
New Year was as far as the eyes
could see!

(137 characters)

Prompt:
To write a Micro Fiction based on the
image and to include the word - *jeopardy*

A Luminous Luminary

Image Deleted:
A young high jumper

Luminous luminary
of a sports personality
Jump specialist he'll be
To sharpen his prowess,
plain to see
At a young age
he's starting early!

(140 characters)

Prompt:
To write a Micro Fiction based on the
image and to include the word - *luminous*

In a drunken stupor!

Image Deleted:
A doctor examining a patient
with his stethoscope

I hear voices in a drunken stupor
It's funny! We doctors can sometimes
'see' the future just by listening
I advise you not to go on drinking

(140 characters)

Prompt:
To write a Micro Fiction based on the
image and to include the word - *stupor*

A Hot-Dog Dog

Image Deleted:
A dog dressed up like
a walking hot-dog

Not that vacant look
You are looking smart
Brace up, you are not
just a dog but a hot-dog
dog. Get it! A walking
hot-dog! Can't you see?

(140 characters)

Prompt
To write a Micro Fiction based on
the image and to include the word - *vacant*

Thanksgiving Jitters

Image Deleted:
A pair of turkeys
awaiting slaughter

Knowing what's coming
is frightening. Why can't
they get it over with
Waiting is annoying

It gets on my nerves
It borders on intimidation!

(140 characters)

Prompt:
To write a Micro Fiction based on the image
and to include the word - *border*

A Special Guest

Image Deleted:
A jail cell

In search of tenants
short or life term young
or old. Under protective
umbrella. Free board and
lodgings. Expect good
service. Call anytime

(140 characters)

Prompt:
To write a Micro Fiction based on the
image and to include the word - *umbrella*

Dark Shadows

Image Deleted:
A dark neighborhood

Dark shadows darting
from house to house in
the cool of the night
Noted for their quick
movements but are they
of suspicious intentions?

(140 characters)

Prompt:
To write a Micro Fiction based on
the image and to include the word - *noted*

To Your Future

Image Deleted:
A boy blowing a horn walking towards
a signboard with the word 'Future'

Blowing his own trumpet
To herald his journey into the future
on his own strength
No necessity to outwit anyone
Friends can come in handy!

(140 characters)

Prompt:
To write a Micro Fiction based on the
image and to include the word - *outwit*

Part IV

Limericks

A Limericks has 5 lines. Lines 1, 2 and 5 are of longer lines and all the 3 lines rhyme together. Lines 3 and 4 are of shorter length and the 2 lines rhyme together but not with the other 3 lines. Limericks are normally witty in nature with lots of humor

The pressure was taking its toll
His confidence was in being bold
Took it in his stride
With all impending pride
Despite him being on the dole

*

A woman was thrilled with her find
Something she wanted all the time
She was happy
Needn't be angry
No more tantrums, tears nor whines

*

A fellow was wearing a suit
All nicely lined looking cute
Very happily
Unabashedly
And he was wearing high boots!

*

A fellow who quite often spoke ill...
Of those others around to his fill
It was unwise
Was ostracized
Had to stop his rumor-mongering mill

*

A fellow who needed a loan
Searched frantically on his own
Had some leads
But not for keeps
Could just render some big moans

They can give whatever bad review
Makes no difference none too few
Up the ante
At your bay
Have to reckon with a stronger you

*

They look like happy know-alls
A convention of odd couples
Better being happy
Than being nasty
There's so much to share in all

*

Some really weird fashion sense
Not to be caught in such trends
Being conservative
Is an alternative
Plain and simple shirt and pants

*

Nursery rhymes and all the fun
Spell-bound for the young 'uns
Formative years
Without the tears
Prepared them well in the long run!

*

Sleeping with the one eye closed
It's an unusual way of trying to doze
Can't be helped
Head will snap
One can't be sure if friends or foes

Seen that spin many times, 'Grand Sale'
Trying to hoodwink, with something stale
But the gullible fell for it
Sellers invariably succeed
A bluff gleefully thrown in on a large scale

*

Being pessimistic, optimistic or realistic
Gets one to think of what really will mix
Ignorance is bliss
Not to give it a miss
Instead think of what to fix that will stick

*

Some are dressed up for the kill
That should plainly fit the bill
They have ideas
Have no fears
Shows a longing long to be fulfilled

*

Peace had never been given a chance
Instead peace had been made to plunge
Down in the abyss
Just pseudo bliss
Security was similar to being in the dumps

*

Dirty or not still lots of laughs
Kind of goings-on that are tough
Take it one at a time
It's all so sublime
Then no one will consider it daft

She can sure cook up something
Would not put in much thinking
Think of something nice
Forget what she had spiced
Not to worry just one of those things

*

Some really weird fashion sense
Not to be caught in such bland
Being conservative
Is an alternative
Plain and simple shirt and pants

*

Yep, just like Larry, Curly and Moe
Many such jokers along the sea-shore
As one can obviously see
Takes little to make them happy
Distance them before they ask for more

*

With all the ramifications
And the standard allusions
A vacation
sanctioned
Rightly the expected solution

*

A pink lunch box gets all the attention
She had made her choice in all innocence
She has every right
With something bright
Putting some color with that Barbie stance!

A chameleon's tongue is longer than itself
I know of some that are sharper than knives
Remain calm facing these
Nothing like being at ease
Sharp tongues toss aside rather have sharp eyes

*

Odd looking signs were hilarious
They appeared dumb that's obvious
Were they meant as jokes
For all kinds of folks
Sure made them all delirious!

*

To get some attention try to be outlandish
May not get a croc but may still land a fish
A matter of showdown
A lift up the crown
Mindful of still some protein left for a dish

*

Hold on tight to your rights
It's certainly not a blight
Others go wild
With their wiles
Maintain yours sunny and bright

*

You can just do your own thing
Don't bother what others think
But don't antagonize
That will be most wise
Stay on your own side and sing

A woman who'd swim in the buff...
Created some unexpected laughs
She tried the backstroke
That was when they broke
Into laughter seeing turfs above

*

A fellow who makes many trips
Feels guilty for he often sleeps
Wakes up with a grunt
For missing the fun
By nature he just can not help it

*

A fellow who frequently trips
Is so clumsy with such a habit
Knocks into tables
Upset lots of people
Grins but not bothered one bit

*

A fellow would constantly hum...
Most of all when on the run
Had my fun
Who's the one
To bother to ask silly questions?

*

A woman who often made scenes...
Could not care for being so mean
Got her own back
When was laughed at
Pity didn't seem to learn anything

A woman was speaking in jest...
Of her objections and loud protests
Reluctantly accepted
By those aggravated
At least it did not end up in a mess

*

A man was enjoying some strips
Original cartoons he used to quip
A collector's fare
Some quite rare
Secured few from change alley trips

*

A man who was driving a truck
Passing some marshes he got stuck
Cursed his luck
Not being a duck
Better off somewhere playing pucks

*

Corporate guys do not depend on luck
Spending time waiting for the big bucks
Things they devise
Makes one despise
Knowing the game they play it sucks

*

With all the great song titles
One can get seemingly muddled
When Johnny B Good
Gets into the mood
One gets all rocking and unsettled

Year-end resolutions to target a bigger number
End of the year upon totaling up they did discover
In terms of percentage
What were achieved
Not 100% success but some parts targeted for

*

Target more people in their own language
Belies well for those for their own usage
Extend the horizon
on familiar Amazon
'Cast the net far and wide' is a good adage

*

It's good and expected for one to be punctual
To arrive before the appointed time is essential
If there is no clock
It's the life of a dog
Shoved around and but pushed and jostled

*

Have fun so says he
Can never better be
Run
Jump
Whatever be happy

*

Snowfall may be such a bother if these are aplenty
None at our equatorial shores where it is a novelty
It can be chore
Shoveling snow
Enjoy the fun when blessed with it and play it easy

Santa, mistletoe, presents, reindeer
Christmas comes early this year?
There're lots of sizzles
With Christmas sales
Let's see what will there be on offer

*

Innovative, brave Christmas deco
That many will rightly crave for
They get the good ones
When shopping for some
But the witty ones will ask for more!

*

Everyone is on a roll, it's Christmas Eve
Festivities already started see what gives
Merry Christmas
And all the Best
Safe driving not too much booze if you please

*

Merry Christmas to you Moms and Dads
Had been a good year with all the spats
For the ensuing year
Make it a real holler
With daring and dazzling pin-falls on the mat

*

Boxing Day with all expectant looks
Presents galore stuck in your nook
Young and old
With same goal
Chalking up lots of boxes are no fluke!

The busybodies having their fun
For them it is just some fine run
They're just creeps
Better off asleep
They're a bother with their rants

*

Yes, it's no fun if one is to yell
Turn around with nothing to tell
It will soon cease
Nothing to please
Life goes on as usual sure as hell

*

A face with no name
What a crying shame
No dice
Stay wise
Focus and go for fame

*

In the maze one gets stuck
Not one to have such luck
Lame duck
On a lark
Good game of passing the buck

*

A fellow with too much red ink
Trying hard to get a direct link
To his accountant
It was just blatant
Never thought his accounts stink

What can be done with just shoe laces
Got to have those already stolen replaced
Women's shoes
Come in all hues
There are a lot of choice you'll be amazed

*

Movie buff that you really are
Not being home but doors ajar
Instead relaxed
At the cineplex
In the neighborhood not that far

*

Threats are just that, they stay as threats
Not to utter so they'll accord respect
In the long run
Fizzled and done
None to bother to cause much impact

*

Going through all the bother
For what, just to save a dollar
Part of the fun
For everyone
Many odd things to clamor for

*

Rules are made to be broken
In jest but rarely heard spoken
Gets on the nerves
Gets one on the toes
But as long as things do function

I'm not supposed to tell
But still they get to smell
Something juicy
Something fishy
But it does not ring a bell

*

Twitter message appears dumb
Too brief and lacks explanation
Don't be fooled
It's just a tool
To get back at others with sarcasm

*

Get banished to the back lawn
Gets one to unnecessarily frown
What of it
Just face it
Don't evaporate, just a little down

*

Dec 2013, it's Friday the 13th
Watch the date, it's rarely seen
Is it unlucky
Yes it can be
Just try to avoid sticky scenes

*

It was over before it began
Rug pulled from under his pants
Very unlucky
Case to be
Trust him to act like a man

The lot of those folks were gullible
Took in anything without trouble
Happy as they please
Unaware of being fleeced
Until thumbed hard and crumpled

*

Creatures with black rings around the eye?
Who would rather want that one for a try!
One got questioned
On one's intentions
Ended up making an exit quietly on the sly

*

Ideas come real and quick
Gives him such a big kick
If it is that easy
What of his energy?
It's bubbling fluid and big!

*

Sue them hard and you would know
And pick those with lots of dough
Lots of embarrassment
With lots of harassment
The vultures would not be that slow

*

They managed to include the lot
Idiomatic slant all the way so hot
Was for good reading
Good for the hearing
Raised higher the finesse one slot

Simple in fact it is too easy
But for others to make money
They create a spin
One will never win
Fraudsters laughing gleefully

*

What of getting stuck in a tree
Watching crowd below walking gaily
Certainly some fun
For those who want
Staying above ground is heavenly

*

In Bedrock Flinstone could still survive
Not to bother but just live a good life
Barney and Dino
Those in the know
Extended him support to remain alive

*

Where else everything's nicely rhyme
Special treat and that's not a crime
He is just there
Snug at his lair
Faithfully rhyming away daily in time

*

Could not really see what's the big title
Clues wanting and remained befuddled
Would just have to wait
Hoping for something great
They sure had ways of being subtle

One were to bother what was said
Wouldn't be any for what was laid
Plug the ears
Have no fears
Cool it one's terms wouldn't fade

*

A girl in an elegant wrap
Envisioned a rich guy to grab
Made herself pretty
A sultry of a lady
But stalked instead by an old jab

*

A woman who thought she needed a fix…
Devised ways to make her looks slick
Worked on all gaiety
But made no money
Despite being dressed as a pretty chick

*

Christmas comes early seems likely enough
Nothing's unusual with people you trust
A Christmas sale in August
Give a try of one so robust
May well just turn out to be a great farce

*

Having gone down the rabbit hole
Was a great adventure in the fold
Meeting a Mad Hatter
Queen that slaughters
Alice had been strong and overly bold

How they love to hoodwink
Those who don't really think
As can be seen
They're the same
The 'ads' people with their spin

*

Boxing Day with all expectant looks
Presents galore stuck in your nook
Young and old
With same goal
Chalking up lots of boxes are no fluke!

*

Eye Rhyming is greatly spectacular
Spelling right but sounds peculiar
Getting to be
Sounds easy
Not easily matched but pairing is a bother

*

Looking around and vying for a date
There're lots of 'choices' at any rate
Travel and unravel
Scraping the barrel
Sealed without success that's the fate

*

Imagine right in your tummy there are worms
Your guts unseen but your stomach squirms
Throwing up action
Is just one option
Better yet replace the tummy as a solution

278

Eye Rhyming is greatly spectacular
Spelling right but sounds peculiar
Getting to be
Sounds easy
Not easily matched as pairing is a bother

*

Looking around and vying for a date
There're lots of 'choices' at any rate
Travel and unravel
Scraping the barrel
Sealed without success that's the fate

*

Those were the days, the era of things bulky
When viewed now they look to be so unwieldy
Time savings when first appeared
Innovative, life changing as touted
But now somehow they are a laugh, real funny

*

It is just no fun when one is out of sync
One acts the fool others enjoy the scene
Getting to grips
On 'mystery' trips
Even raging mad will not mean a thing

*

Give them back more than just a hint
They never realize they cause a din
A crooning
Out of sync
Making it known, at least they try to sing

Happy Fourth nice people there
Fireworks and all wonderful fare
To rejoice
Just as much
Make it fun and games everywhere

*

Chased by the wind and they zoomed pass
Got us wondering why the need to be fast
We might just meet them
At the very next turn
Curled and smashed for they just don't last

*

A little 'mermaid' is something challenging
But they ought to learn to stop arguing
Give way a little
When it's bearable
They can pool resources and end up winning

*

Greed of the traders knows no bounds
They bid to suck from everyone around
All ways they sieve
Lots up their sleeve
One is left saddened with lots of frowns

*

Just amazing what people might do
Not realizing when focused on you
At least cover up
When not in the dark
Bad luck when seen in full view

Part V

Forms for All

It comprises many different forms of poetry such as Tanka, Sonnets,Tetractys and many others .These are of lesser numbers and are grouped together. The definition of each one of them will be at the top of the poem

A Wish - Collum Lune

Note: This is a 3-5-3 words Collum Lune
The lune is also known as the American haiku in an
either a 5-3-5 *syllabic* form or a 3-5-3 *words* form
Here it is the 3-5-3 words form

Make a wish
Fabric of imagination found wanting
Septic idle thoughts

Discard puerile attitude
Mind propelled source of strength
when wisely harnessed

Stimulant to wonders
Benefiting mankind to be expected
But detractors exist

Human conflicts, commercial
exploitation, family strife, robbery, murder
minimized or shackled

Greed and self-interest
Upset the equation, if only
mankind is forgiving!

Feeding Time - A Cinquain

Note: A Cinquain has a
syllabic count of 2-4-6-8-2

Image Deleted:
Feeding giraffe at the Giraffe Center

Ho-hum!
Where are they now?
Normally on time, ah
finally! Need to stretch my neck
for this!

Image Deleted:
Feeding a Camel in a Zoo

Thirsty?
No! Hungry? yes!
Not complaining but lots
of food in the Zoo and just a
morsel?

Image Deleted:
Feeding a seal after
a performance

Feeding
motivates. An
incentive to react
Trainers reward good performance
It works

Post Vacation Blues - A Sijo

Note1: A Sijo, a Korean form of
poetry has three lines. Each line
has 14-16 syllables for a total
count of between 44-46 syllables.

The first line introduces the theme,
the second develops the theme in a different direction
and the final line provides closure or
in other words,
a thesis, development and conclusion

Back from vacation, tiresome and disoriented (15 syllables) - *thesis*
But it seems it is normal in the initial few days or so (16 syllables) - *development*
Brimming with feelings of freshness after that and it is true (15 syllables) – *conclusion*

(46 syllables)

Note2: Hank just come back
from a 2- week vacation

Stormy Encounter - Dada Poem

Note: Dada Poems with Scissors.
We are to select a text and get it cut
up and rearranged to form a poem.

Process Note: A press report of a storm
warning was used as the base text. Hank
had it truncated, 'cut up' and re-arranged.
It turned out to be disjointed before words
were inserted in between to make it
presentable.

His resolve was expected to weaken
into a hurricane of emotions
It could spawn in his heart tornadoes
of feel to cause flooding of tears of despair
outwardly seen as a storm surge
before it lost its strength

They were in effect leading to a
confrontation for a large section of his soul

He was in control however despite storm warnings
haggling for his love amid storm conditions
It was expected somewhere close to his insides
It was a resurgence of the area of disaster
within a clear-headed self in a day and a half.

Rains and winds swept northwards into his head
Seeking refuge on the shelf of safety and
were not expected to lose steam

It closed the road to any redundant reconciliation
that yanked at sympathetic ears and the mind that
frequently were flooded with denial during
heavy uplifts of stormy encounters

Soaked unsparingly in part and skidding along
swirling waters damaging to his reputation
he reluctantly moved on!

The Haze - A Sedoka

Note: A Sedoka is a Japanese form
that has a 5-7-7 syllabic count

Getting on with it
Things had been on a roll with
harmonious happenings

Same cannot be said
of local haze position
Threw everything off tangent

Outdoor events were
cancelled visibility
was bad. Health hazard warnings

What happened to the

Dinosaurs? - An Anaphora

Note: An Anaphora is where the word
commencing a *line* or a *stanza* is the same
throughout

What happened to the carefree days
when time stood still and childhood
innocence governed ways of laughter
but disappeared even before it started

What happened to the environment
now long polluted choking the
waterways and the green-house effects
spelled danger above

What happened to the neighborhood
unsafe except for gangland packs
roving the streets made easy for them
and law enforcement rendered ineffective

What happened to the growing up years of
physical activities for sporting
prowess now acquiesced taken over
by FB and on-line preferences indoors

What happened to all the grown-ups
embattled to survive in trying times
of economic hardships and exploitation
perpetrated by big business

What happened to the ever mystifying question
left unanswered on the whys and wherefores
of disappearance of dinosaurs which could
have been an unending supply chain (chuckles) of meat

What happened, people?

Music by Karunesh - a Tanka

Note: A Tanka is a Japanese form
that has a 5-7-5-7-7 syllabic count

Beauty of testing
desert living a Spartan
way of existence
Listening intently yet
Unfazed of the searing heat

Prompt:
A music video by Karunesh
that has a Middle Eastern
touch was provided

Space to Move - An etheree

Note: An etheree is a form that progressively
increases in syllable count from one to ten

Space
One needs
more than just
Space to muster
Efforts and gumption
to burst out from the chest
So much to rally round that
one is not strong enough to snuff
Need to react positively to
friendly banter with friends and foes alike

Prompt:
Space

Wonders of The Universe - Twitter Poetry

Image Deleted:
Jupiter as Seen in Space

Note: A twitter message is more or less
standardized to 140 characters akin to
a micro fiction

The wonders of the Universe
Movements on its own momentum
An inertia driven witnessed
in light years from a distance
A clock-work precision

Jupiter not naked eyes
can peek from afar
but with telescopic help
Sighted rings of dust!
Artistically inclined
Revolving every ten hours

(Each stanza is of 140 characters)

Happiness is Infectious - A Tetractys

Note: A Tetractys comprises at least 5 lines
of 1 2 3 4 and 10 syllables (total of 20)
It can be written with more than one verse
but must follow suit with an inverted
syllable count

Grins
Happy
as can be
Wonderful smiles
And truly it is very infectious
There are many things to worry about
Make no mistake
Smiling wide
will solve
them!

Smile
Easy
does it, man
And no holds barred
But many tried and failed miserably
There is sure way to stake reality?
Yes, certainly
Open arms
sincere
hugs!

The Slick and Sly - Senryu

Image Deleted:
Modern Day Street Hustlers

Note1: Senryu are of a 5-7-5 syllable count
similar to haiku but with a slight difference
(the word senryu and haiku have no plural
forms)

Note2: This is what Wiki has to say of Senryu

"Senryū tend to be about human foibles
while haiku tend to be about nature,
and senryū are often cynical or darkly
humorous while haiku are more serious."
A very fine difference

Slick and sly, smiling
to himself confidently
He stood unobserved

Sizing up the crowd
with a cursory glance he
worked out his move

Seeing a likely
dope he was quick to react
with his weapons drawn

Ensnared the poor thing
did not have a chance. Victim
of the smooth talker

Prompt:
smooth

Endorsement of Perfection - A Tanka

Image Deleted:
Flying Rock Dove

Note: A Tanka has a syllable
count of 5-7-5-7-7

Flapping wings of doves
Ushering whispers of success
Winds of emotions
Haggling for warmth of friendship
Secured through strenuous efforts

Spirits of youth smiled
Despite conflicts encountered
Strength of character
Triumphant yet again pending
endorsement of perfection

Tummy Pains Determined – A Pensee

Note: A Pensee has a 2-4-7-8-6
syllable count whereby

line one is the subject line,
line 2 is description,
line 3 is action
line 4 is setting and
line 5 is the final thoughts on the poem

Gastric
Lingering pain
Endoscopy check performed
Ulcers confirmed but not serious
Ailment is now addressed

Relationships - Fibonacci Poems

Note: A Fibonacci has a number series
of 1- 1- 2- 3- 5- 8-13-21…. syllable count
but can stop at any point

Joy
Fun
Two souls
Together
What can be better
Life is for the asking give love
Rewards and care can come together and never fail
Many such sincere relationships have been blessed for all their wonderful attitudes

Dastardly Delinquent - A Huitain

The original huitain is a single verse eight
line poem with eight syllables per line. The
rhyme scheme is *a b a b b c b c*. When it
was adapted into English, the same rhyme
scheme was retained but 10 or 8 syllables

were used per line. There was no alternation
between the syllable count. The huitain was
all of 10 or all of 8 syllables

Hank had chosen to do the 10 syllable count
and also tried to be a little naughty by employing
alliterations with letters *d* and *b*

a dreaded dreary disorientated
b definitely dastardly delinquent
a dislodged dismantled and dissipated
b dwindled to defenseless delirium
b but balanced boldness brought benevolence
c besieged bondage but bizarre bravado
b began to beat and bash those beholden
c brutal beastly barrage like a bronco

Note: The above revolved around a delinquent
Tom cat that was ill-treated but later fought back

Friday, October 4, 2013

Never Had it so Good! - A Sedoka

Image Deleted:
Autumn Leaves

Note: A sedoka has 2 stanzas
of a 5-7-7 syllable count

Anger raving mad
What, summer fleetingly gone?
Gosh, never had it so good!

What do I see now?
Brown unsmiling looking trees!
Cannot wait for White Christmas

Preference for Flowers - a Cinquain

Note: A Cinquian is a poem of 5 lines with a
syllable count of 2, 4, 6, 8, 2. In its restrictive
form it may even be expected to be as follows:

First line: a one-word subject or title.
Second line: two adjectives which describe the subject.
Third line: three verbs relating to the subject.
Fourth line: four words forming a phrase, sentence,
or set of feelings relating to the subject.
Fifth line: one word which summarizes the
poem or restates the subject.

But here it is the easier option of
maintaining just the syllable count

Conflicts
Ever present
Found in line of fire
Women and children young and old
Pity

Flowers
Soothing effects
Nature's wonder of peace
Colors do propagate beauty
Dainty

Regal Bearing - Trireme sonnet

Image Deleted:
An Ewe, Lambs and a Heron Beside a Lake

Note1: A Trireme sonnet has 14 lines of 8 or
10 syllables for each line (10 syllables in this
case) It has four tercets (3 lines) with a rhyme
scheme of abc-abc-abc-abc followed by a
couplet (two lines) of an aa rhyme scheme

Note2: A sonnet can comprise three quatrains
(four lines)and a couplet (two lines) or of four
tercets and a couplet (and as in this case and
it is called a Trireme sonnet)

Note3: Another restriction for sonnets is to
conform to iambic pentameter which relates
to unstressed/stressed syllable pairings. It is
a little complicated to conform with and it is
ignored here (as well as in all of the other
sonnets following this)

a Standing tall majestically well-bred
b Mother's call stamped authoritatively
c Within proximity a protector

a Where a heron is considered a threat
b Sauntering a regal pose glaringly
c Undaunted unflinching all to savor

a Fluffed coat of noble breeding suavely decked
b Furtively fragrant and impeccably
c placed blessings rightly procured to endure

a Ewe vibrant unwilling to segregate
b Gregarious thriving nature of fairly
c accepted friendship a sober gesture

a Young lambs of safely groomed family trait
a An outlandish future cautiously made

Being Thankful - Shakespearian Sonnet

Note: A Shakespearian sonnet is of 14 lines with
end rhymes of a-b-a-b, c-d-c-d, e-f-e-f, g-g while
maintaining the 10-syllable count for each line

a Creating desire to be thankful
b Many are taken with such noble thoughts
a They make a real effort to be grateful
b and to register very well their lot

c Sadly ingrates persist not to bother
d Begged for help to later disappear
c No conscience and took it as small matter
d Favors from others do not register

e Is it a weakness of one's character
f To succumb to sob stories easily
e Only to realize being duped later
f By the unscrupulous and paid dearly

g It may hurt but for poetic justice
g is an equalizer without malice

On Being Nice - Terza Rima Sonnet

Note: A Terza Rima sonnet is a rhyming poetry
written in tercets - ie three-line stanzas and ends
with a couplet. It has a strict rhyming structure of
aba bcb cdc ded ee. The 10-syllable count in each
of the 14 lines is maintained here

a Never in his wildest dreams had he known
b Destined to be witness of vanity
a Demonstrated by the sullen who frowned

b Though devoid of acts of indignity
c Startled and intensely incoherent
b Blabbering to no end unashamedly

c Why insist to willfully abandon
d politeness and sense of good upbringing
c and forgetting judicious indulgence

d Shouts of 'simpleton' just kept on ringing
e Much to embarrassment of those present
d Ethics and etiquette thrown to the winds

e Painful and sorely it was a lesson
e To be enlightened sane and elegant

Merry Christmas - A Kyrielle Sonnet

Image Deleted:
A Christmas Tree with Lighted
Candles and Presents

A Kyrielle Sonnet
It comprises 14 lines of three rhyming
quatrain stanzas and a couplet. Just as
the traditional Kyrielle, the sonnet here
also has a repeating line as a refrain. It
appears as the last line of each stanza
The eight syllables per line is maintained
The rhyming scheme is AabB ccbB ddbB AB

Wishing everyone Merry Christmas
and Happy Holidays

A Bright star surveying down below
a Colorful lights and mistletoe
b Stand below it,'care for a kiss'
B Hail to the Yuletide cheer and more

c Standing a pine tree green and lean
c From Wal Mart gramps carried it in
b Tinsel swaying in a slight breeze
B Hail to the Yuletide cheer and more

d Santa sneaks in with the presents
d Demands from young hearts more brazen
b Expensive items are their wish
B Hail to the Yuletide cheer and more

A Parents relent expenses soar
B Merry Christmas Happy New Year